For my amazing family:
Please do yourself a favor
and do not read this.

1. PEACHES

My grandmother, Mumma, taught me the meaning of true, unconditional love. By this, I am not at all saying that she showed me the profound power of love or any shit like that. No, what I mean is that Mumma was a devout Hindu who was also severely racist and homophobic to a fault—but I loved her (and still do) more than anyone or anything.

In the fall of 2006, my grandparents took my brother and me to New Jersey for the first interracial wedding in our extended family. I was ecstatic because, even at that age, I was acutely aware that I already had a preference for lean white meat. Moreover, this wasn't just an interracial wedding—it was a HinJew wedding. My aunt was marrying a Jewish man and there would be a Hindu ceremony followed by a traditional Hebrew wedding.

As I prattled on during the 17-hour road trip about all of the Hebrew traditions we would be able to witness, Mumma proceeded to continuously pop her blood pressure medication like they were Tic Tacs. Meanwhile, Dadaji's eyebrows furrowed more and more until they just became one unibrow disdainfully looking at me from the rearview mirror.

My enthusiasm was quickly squashed once I realized that my grandparents had no intention of going to the Hebrew ceremony that was taking place after the

Hindu ceremony. I pouted and asked to go, but Mumma insisted we would just take the extra time to get ready for the reception.

The reception was an even bigger buzzkill. Being 15 at the time, I couldn't drink and was stuck at the table with the senior citizens while my brother, Marco, ditched me for some new friends he had made.

Nobody comes to weddings to make friends, I remember bitterly thinking to myself. *You come to weddings to hang out with people you know and make fun of the bozos that you don't know* (in my later years, I would become one of those bozos).

I sat there sipping my virgin margarita as I plotted my exit so that I could make it to the hotel room in time for reruns of *The Golden Girls*. I glanced over at Mumma and gave a look of exasperation. As the happy couple danced their first dance together, Mumma was slumped over in her chair like she had just found out *General Hospital* had been pulled off the air.

"Are you okay?" I asked, already knowing the answer.

"*Beta*," Mumma said, suddenly turning to me with a renewed vigor and gazing at me intensely. "Promise me you will never marry a BMW."

Beads of sweat formed on her forehead as I took in Mumma's serious expression. She continued to exuberantly fan herself with a cocktail napkin.

"A BMW?" I asked, perplexed. "Of course not. Indian people only buy white Mercedes."

"No," Mumma said, in a seriously tone. "BMW. No blacks, Muslims, or whites."

"So...Latino men are still on the table?" I asked, after a beat. "I do love their food—and their butts."

I was promptly smacked on the head and I proceeded to cackle like the wicked witch in a children's book.

In May 2012, President Barack Obama declared same-sex marriage to be a civil right. Mumma was in for another rude awakening. As she sat there on the recliner and watched the news, I came up and said, in an upbeat voice, "Isn't this great?"

Mumma looked at me and had the same forlorn expression on her face that she had at the HinJew wedding.

"No," she told me, gravely concerned. "This is not good."

Having never broached the subject of homosexuality with her, I gave a quizzical look. "Why not?"

"These people have a sickness," Mumma said. "It's a disease of the mind. The president shouldn't be supporting this."

Mumma looked so deeply concerned about an issue that didn't affect her in the slightest and was staring at me with eyes that implored me to see her reasoning. I gave Mumma a long, hard look.

"Well," I said slowly, "What if I wanted to marry a woman? Or Marco wanted to marry a man? Would that mean that we have diseased minds?"

Mumma swiftly smacked me on the arm and said, "*Chee, gandi*," essentially calling me the equivalent of a dirty girl.

That was the end of that conversation.

These two stories are still a highlight at most dinner parties I go to (as long as they are not attended by the family). The truth is, most Indian people who are Generation X or older are inherently racist, but they will never admit to being bigoted. Rather, they will make comments such as BMW and say the Indian equivalent of the n-word, while still talking about discrimination against Indian people in America.

Whenever I asked my relatives if they considered themselves to be racist or homophobic, they would always promptly say, "No." Following this, I would immediately ask them if they were okay with me marrying somebody of another race or the same gender, to which they would respond, "No, but it's not racist/homophobic. Those people just don't understand our culture and values."

Based on these conversations, all I could gather was that Indian people had this deeply ingrained idea that their own morals and values were much higher than that of people from other cultures. I would later learn that this was false and that older generations in Indian families simply have an irrational fear that other cultures and family structures will try to change age-old customs and traditions.

I find this deep-rooted belief slightly ironic and close-minded given that Indians are the people who invented the Kama Sutra. I was only 14-years-old when my grandmother asked for help unpacking her bags after going on a luxurious cruise with Dadaji. Since Mumma was one of the four people I actually liked, I agreed to help.

I took out Mumma's clothes and started to put them away in her drawers. As I reached for another pile of knitted sweaters, my hand hit something tubular. I picked up the bottle and found what I can only describe as an industrial-sized bottle of K-Y lube. I stared in abject horror as Mumma came up behind me.

"Oh, that," Mumma bashfully said as she quickly grabbed it out of my hand. "That's for my bad arm. I have to massage it in."

I, looking like I had just eaten a menstrual blood flavored jelly bean, made a strangled noise in my throat before turning tail and going to my room. Who was she kidding? Everyone knows what K-Y is for.

....

At 4:35 AM on November 25, 2013, I woke up to this text from my cousin:

Tinu: So sorry to hear about Mumma. If you need anything let me know.

In my groggy state, I read the text, confused, just as I heard a knock from my bedroom door. I quickly slipped on a robe and answered the door. My parents and my aunt were standing in the doorway and I squinted against the light with disgust. My dad, Melvin, told me what I already knew: Mumma had died earlier that morning.

As my family quickly moved in to hug me, my first thought, as usual, was completely inappropriate: *holy shit. My nipples could cut glass right now and this sheer robe is not covering anything. Can everyone please get off of me?*!

Without a tear shed, I mumbled something about having to get ready and closed the door.

I proceeded to take one of the longest showers of my life, running the water until it went ice cold. Most people would think that this was because I was in shock, but, in truth, I knew this was my last shot at a nice, hot shower before the cavalry arrived.

I joined the rest of the family an hour later and I

took a seat with Marco at the breakfast nook. I immediately wondered to myself if I was high. I saw my 15 aunts and uncles pacing the living room and the kitchen as if they were bees swarming the hive. Most of them were on the phone, talking to the hospital, funeral home, and relatives. Several uncles were placing a giant white sheet over the television and placing a small table with a *diyo*, a small Indian candle with ghee instead of wax, in front of it. From the look of it, my aunts were making chai by the bucketload. Several other aunts were raiding the pantry and sorting through the snacks, listing how much was left of each one, like they were rationing food during the Holocaust.

"Hey guys," my cousin, Nick, said as he came in through the front door and offered me a hug. "I'm so sorry, man."

Nick looked extremely stoned, but it was also only 7:00 AM at this point. I gave him the benefit of the doubt (even though, as you will learn in time, Nick should never be given the benefit of the doubt).

After a few minutes of awkward silence with Marco, Nick abruptly stood up and announced, "I need to go to the bathroom."

Nick proceeded to go to the bathroom at the other end of the house with what I can only describe as a turtle-head-stopping walk. Despite the obvious inappropriateness of the situation, Marco and I both snickered quietly.

After a few minutes, both of our phones went off simultaneously. Nick had sent us a group chat.

Nick: Can one of you guys bring a pair of boxers to the bathroom?

Marco and I looked quizzically at one another.

Marco: Why?

After a moment, with no response given, my brother proceeded to grab some boxers and slip them through a crack in the bathroom door as Nick hastily grabbed them from him.

A minute later, we saw Nick emerge from the bathroom with a plastic bag. Wordlessly, Nick went into the garage and threw the bag in the garbage can. Nick then rejoined us at the breakfast nook without a word.

Marco and I stared at Nick with our mouths agape.

"Dude," Marco said. "Did you just shit yourself?"

"Shut up, man, I'm stressed!" Nick abruptly said.

Marco and I proceeded to erupt into a fit of laughter, mimicking, as we are so often told, the hyenas from *The Lion King.*

I never thought that it was possible to laugh again so shortly after the person closest to you passed away. Leave it to an only child like Nick to prove me wrong and take the spotlight away from the deceased within five hours.

....

The funeral was to be held on that following Wednesday, two days later. The family began to pour in, and with it, the ensuing hilarity.

I was charged with finding a picture of my grandmother which would go over the giant sheet-covered television as a makeshift shrine. Being the family klutz, I was also warned that the *diyo* could not be allowed to be unlit during the mourning period.

Great, I thought, *We're just supposed to be okay with this fire hazard? Now we're all going to die in a fiery accident just because one person passed away!*

The morning of the funeral, I spent a few minutes alone near the side of the lawn. This was the first time I cried. As I bawled my eyes out and fell to the grass, at least five neighbors walked by. Through tear streaked curtains, I watched the neighbors stare for a brief moment before averting their gaze and continue to power walk. I decided I needed to do the same and pulled myself together.

My uncle, Neel, was the coordinator for the entire funeral. When it comes to taking charge and bossing people around, even under the saddest of circumstances, he's the guy you want for the job. Neel came out and instructed me to get onto the shuttle.

"What shuttle?" I asked, feigning a sneeze and chalking up my red eyes to the nonexistent pollen in the air.

Neel pointed to the shuttle 20 feet away from me.

"Oh god," I said, appalled, as I looked at an airport shuttle van. "Is that what we're going to the funeral in? It looks like we are headed from the baggage claim at the airport and going to check-in at the Ramada before a sad Disney vacation."

I turned around and Neel was already gone. I resigned myself to a sigh and got on the van. Leave it to Indian people to cheap out and use an airport shuttle van instead of the socially acceptable limo.

Once the van was fully loaded with the family members Neel had assigned to it, I realized how deafening silence could be. The van moved for the next 20 minutes in a stillness so quiet that you could hear the moths on the bus flapping their wings. Finally, my uncle, Ajay, broke the silence.

"It smells like Latinos in here," Ajay said matter-of-factly.

"Hmm," I said, breathing in the faint scent of burritos and Chupa Chups. "Interesting. Very interesting."

Like Nick, Ajay was skilled at taking away attention from the deceased, even en route to their funeral. Based on the glaring looks the rest of the family was giving him, I suspected Ajay's funeral would be next.

"Hey, you guys," Ajay suddenly said, as we continued down the highway. "Did you guys see that billboard?"

We had all of course seen the billboard. We had all been staring out the windows since we left the house, zeroing in on the various billboards and the sad definition of Orlando's skyline, trying to distract ourselves from the coming service.

Despite the silent response, Ajay continued by saying, "It's a church and it said, 'Jesus Welcomes You,' with a picture of a black guy and a blonde woman with giant cans. What do you make of it?"

The silence continued.

When we arrived at the funeral home, I had it completely together. Then I saw Mumma. I can only describe what happened next as a complete shutdown of my body. I collapsed and my cousin, Pri, had to hold me up on one side while my aunt, Pari, held me up on the other. I made it to the viewing area and sat down as I basically continued to break down in giant, blubbering sobs that would not stop.

Indian funerals are particularly traumatizing, even in America. The men of the family rub ghee on the feet of the deceased. I sat there watching as my brother and Melvin did this and then had to wait my turn to touch the feet. There is nothing quite as disturbing as touching the cold feet of your stiff grandmother and then being unable to get the smell of formaldehyde off of your hands until the funeral is over. Seeing as I was not in any condition to make a speech, my brother made one instead. I still don't remember anything that was said during the speech thanks to my hysterical sobbing.

Once the actual funeral is over, the men of the family carry the casket to the crematorium and the entire family follows. Somehow, despite wanting to maintain a distance, I was pushed towards the front. There are only a few funeral homes within Florida that allow Indian people to do this. We watched the body as it went into the flames and then close. I still have never forgotten the heat from that, nor the fact that I couldn't help but wonder, *Wow. The guy working the crematorium must have great skin. This heat must exfoliate the shit out of him, no wonder he looks so well preserved.*

....

Indians like to do everything bigger and better than anybody else. Indian weddings alone are a week long (not including the two weeks of partying beforehand), and Diwali, Indian New Year's, is five days at a minimum. Therefore, it's no surprise that when it comes to death, Indians take a full 13 days after the cremation to complete the mourning period.

During these 13 days, my life became a living hell. You would think that this anguish was because I just lost the most important person in my life—no, it was because of the cavalry's arrival a.k.a my entire extended family.

Indians mourn the exact opposite of how I imagine the Irish mourn. During the mourning period, no meat is allowed within the house, and it's basically some version of the same RDBS (*rotli, dal, bhat, shak*, which is just bread, lentil soup, rice, and vegetables) every night. Additionally, there is absolutely no drinking allowed. The only ones who had a harder time with no alcohol during this period were mostly likely all of my uncles, who were missing their nightly pours of J&B. Even worse than the lack of imbibing was the fact that my house was packed with over 15 people and absolutely none of them had any sense of personal space.

While our house was normally spacious at five bedrooms and four bathrooms, there were a minimum of three relatives crammed in each room. With more relatives arriving each day, I grew concerned about my own accommodations. After initially holding on to my room for the first few days, Pri and I were eventually exiled to the den. It was at this point that I became increasingly bitter. I knew that I was in dangerous territory and that these were not normal circumstances.

Despite the fact that myself, Pri, Marco, and my other cousin, Pavit, were secretly up until 3:00 AM drinking on most nights, I made it my own personal mission to ensure that I was up at 6:00 AM on the dot everyday to beat all of the old biddies to the showers. You see, my grandfather's sisters had taken over the realm and they would probably flog me with their wooden canes in order to beat me to the shower. If I didn't get to the showers before their breakfast time, I would be forced to wait until all of the elders had their turn first. I was suffering enough emotionally and I was not about to let my personal hygiene take a toll.

At 6:00 AM on that first day of mourning, I turned off my alarm and quietly walked towards the bathroom.

My great aunt was coming out of the bathroom at this time. I stared at her in the darkness, like a tiger hunting its prey. My eyes narrowed. *That old biddy has figured out my game.* As soon as she made it back to her (MY) room, I quickly slipped into the bathroom.

My head was pounding from the bottle of wine I guzzled down a few hours prior to. *It really isn't my fault that I drank so quickly,* I reasoned. *I had to use my Book of Mormon coffee mug and I can't be expected to drink slowly from that—my body thought it was just coffee!*

As I let the hot water drown out my thoughts, I went to grab my loofah. I froze. The brand new loofah I had just bought was fully soaked and warm. That lady had just used my own personal loofah to scrub her decrepit body.

I did the only rational thing: I puked in the shower, toweled myself off, and threw the loofah in the trash. *Let it stay there,* I thought. *I'll leave it to send a message to the others.* Coincidentally, this is the same strategy I use for cockroaches, letting their carcasses stay out for a day or two to send a warning to their fellow brethren.

I decided to let the loofah thing go for that moment—I had bigger fish to fry: it had been five days since my mouth had had a single bite of meat in it. I was ravenous for a juicy ribeye or a whole roasted pig with an apple in its mouth. I had no appetite for anymore RDBS and needed some protein, stat.

"We need to smuggle a steak into the house," I confided in Marco.

"I think that's a bit unrealistic. How about a burrito?" he thoughtfully offered.

"Deal."

Later that evening, while feigning some excuse

about work to the family, Marco snuck out to the nearest Chipotle. When he returned, the family was gathered in the living room.

"Did you get the goods?" I whispered, trying not to blow the cover on this operation.

"In the fridge," he robotically answered.

"Inside or outside?"

"Outside," Marco confirmed.

"Good. good."

My mom suddenly came up and told Marco and Pavit to take seats at the table. My mom then instructed Pri and I to sit on the floor of the living room.

"What fresh hell is this?" I muttered to Pri, who just gave me a quizzical look in return.

My parents unveiled the TV and put it on an Indian YouTube channel that only played *bhajans*, or Indian hymns. Dadaji's sisters, my great aunts, were all gathered around the living room. That's when I learned what the true meaning of suffering is. All of my great aunts burst out into singing bhajans for the next two hours. My great aunts are truly wonderful people (minus The Loofah Bandit), but they have zero pitch. The "singing" that I heard could only be described as the sound of a bunch of alley cats being drowned in a bag. Every time we thought it was over, another bhajan would begin. It was like I was in the Hindu version of *Groundhog Day*, but much, much worse.

"This is borderline sacrilege," I said to nobody in particular, while really hoping they all heard.

Once the two hours of sheer torture were over, the four of us made a beeline for the garage. Pri, Marco, Pavit, and I scarfed down Chipotle like it was our last meal —which, given the events of the last few days, it really could have been. To this day, I have never had such flavorful meat in my mouth (my apologies to my husband).

Later that night, in a burrito-induced coma, I stumbled to the bathroom to take out my contacts. I entered the bathroom and faced the mirror. My eyes had circles under them as dark as the bottom of a well and my face had aged at least 20 years. *Woof*, I thought, as I reached for the lens solution.

My heart stopped. Sitting on the bathroom counter were a pair of dentures. Sure, I had seen dentures before, like in a case on the bathroom counter. This was different. This was literally a pair of dentures sitting with nothing between them and the countertop, staring at me, with the mouth lining still parted open. I wanted to stop looking but it was like looking into The Eye of Sauron.

"What the fuck!" I yelled, finally summoning the power to get away. I hightailed it back to the den. What's a little bit of conjunctivitis from sleeping in your contacts all night compared to staying another minute with those teeth?

"What's wrong?" Pri mumbled, half asleep on the sleeping bag in the den.

"Can't talk," I flatly said, pulling the covers over me and using my pillowcase to soak up the sweat.

The next morning, I was in rare form.

"Listen up, bozos," I said as I cornered Melvin and his sister, Sana. "We have a problem on our hands."

They both looked at me with dumbfounded curiosity as I recapped the events of the last 24 hours.

"I feel I have suffered enough," I said guilelessly. "It's not enough that my grandmother is dead, but now I have to deal with people using MY loofah and dentures on the bathroom counter?!"

"You know, Sejal," Melvin said, using that same fortune-cookie-wisdom-giving-advice voice that I utterly loathed. "They grew up in a different time. Your grandfather and his sisters didn't grow up as fortunate as you have. For them, its normal to share bars of soap or loofahs—"

"Woah!" I interjected. "Who said anything about sharing bars of soap? What are we, in prison?! I've already stashed away my body wash, thank you."

"Well," Melvin continued, "my point is that this is not unusual. To them, this is just normal and a sign that they are comfortable with their family members to share items like that."

Sana remained silent but, upon one quick glance, I knew she was disturbed, too.

"Well," I said, losing my patience, "I am very *un*-comfortable with the fact that none of these women seem to have any sense of personal boundaries. Not to mention the fact that tonight I will be subject to their incessant caterwauling, again, as they attempt to 'sing.' They're your dad's sisters—get them in line, soldier!"

I stormed away, knowing that the next 12 days would still be full of the same shit.

Over the coming weeks, conditions drastically worsened. The grief in the air had been taken over by the smell of stale farts and mothballs. There was baby oil constantly covering any surface that I tried to sit on, thanks to all of my aunts putting it on their heads, because they believe it helps revitalize hair. I got scolded twice for clipping my nails at night because my great aunts told me that it was considered to be very bad luck.

"Are you kidding me?" I told my great aunt, as she

kept banging on the bathroom door to be let in. "Mumma dropped dead this week and I have a hangnail. I think we've met our quota for bad luck."

"We can't take it anymore," I declared to Melvin, three days later. Pri was stationed at my side. "We need out."

"What do you mean?" Melvin asked, clueless as ever.

"I mean, we need a break from you dummies. I'm a suicide risk thanks to all this 'family time.' This is for our own health. Get us a hotel."

"Sejal, you guys can't just leave the family," Melvin said. "It wouldn't look right."

"Look. Nobody's talking about leaving the family. It's been 23 years and I'm still living 10 feet away from you guys—I got the message loud and clear. I'm talking about one night to reset at a hotel."

Melvin looked at the desperation and insanity in my eyes and reluctantly said, "I'll see what I can do."

Six hours later, Pri and I were in a hotel room 15 minutes away from the house. We snuggled up with piles of paninis and macaroni and cheese along with wine.

....

The annoying part about death is figuring out the logistics after the shock settles in. After the 13 days of mourning concluded, a few stragglers were still in our midst, including my aunt, Sana. Like me, Sana found comfort in taking control and organizing.

In the days following the cavalry's exodus from Brown Town, Sana and I began to sort through Mumma's possessions in order to free up some drawers and compartmentalize the grieving.

"I hope I don't find more lube in one of these drawers," I said as I examined another box of identical red bindis.

"...What?" Sana asked.

I gave Sana the Cliff Notes on my horrific findings from when I last helped to unpack Mumma's possessions.

"Why did you have to tell me that?!" Sana asked, half laughing, half mortified.

"Well, she's your mom. If I had to be traumatized by it then I prefer that you do, too."

I opened the bottom drawer to find a stack of folders. As I opened the folders, I found remnants of what had been a great legacy. There were articles of Mumma's donations to various charities and her work that she had done volunteering. I leafed through the pages, taking it all in, until something made me pause.

"What the..."

"What?" Sana asked.

I handed her the biodata sheet I had found. For those of you unfamiliar, a biodata sheet is basically a dating résumé that Indian parents hand out to prospective suitors. Biodata sheets usually include the person's education, achievements, religion, skin color, family lineage, and a picture of themselves. For reference, I have attached my prospective biodata sheet below:

BASIC INFORMATION

Name: Sejal Patel

Location: My parent's house

State: Gujarat

Religion: No, thank you.

Diet: Lean white meat preferred, but I will occasionally indulge in the dark meat.

PHYSICAL DESCRIPTION
Height: Just like TI likes his ladies, 5'6"
Body Type: Picture an upside-down pear
Skin Color: Melt-In-Your-Mouth Caramel

Parental Occupations:
Melvin Patel: Something in hotels with spreadsheets.
BB Patel: She makes samosas

About Me:
I am a perfect cross between Wednesday Addams and a really flamboyant gay man. I have an extremely unfortunate personality but I make up for it with a mediocre body. I don't talk, I squawk. My psychiatrist says that I am a borderline sociopath, but, and I quote, "...Don't worry, we're just going to keep an eye on that." I am looking for a man who likes long walks on the beach followed by an even longer happy hour. I like my men like I like my wine—big, bold, and finely aged.

Skills:

- Sass Mouth: 5/5
- Game of Thrones Trivia: 4/5
- Taraji P. Henson: 5/5
- Cooking: 3/5
- Drinking Wine: 5/5

The biodata sheet I found was for my single aunt who was in her late 30s and lived in Nairobi. Mumma's side of the family is host to a couple of feminist aunts that have never been married but are all wildly successful and big boozers. The thing that struck me was that this biodata sheet was up-to-date until two months prior, including her age and current employer.

"Oh my god," I said, rifling through the papers. "It's

like she had these bulk-copied at Kinko's! Do you think she was still giving these out when she would go to India?"

"Probably," Sana said, with no note of surprise.

"Jesus, do you think that's what she was doing with all those wallet-size photos she made me get of myself?"

"Most likely," Sana said, still not sounding the least bit shocked.

Two years earlier, my family went to the respectable establishment that is Sears to have family portraits done. At one point, Mumma and Dadaji insisted that Marco and I each get a separate headshot done. I found the request strange, as nobody else had done their own headshots, but I figured I was cute and of course my grandmother wanted a picture of just me. When the pictures were delivered a few weeks later, I noticed that there were about 30 individual wallet-size photos of just me and the same went for my brother. I was immediately suspicious.

I pushed the thought of my 21-year-old wallet-size photo being handed around Gujarat like party favors. I put the biodata sheets into the junk pile and continued to go through the files. That's when I found my next gem: a letter from Mumma to Melvin when he was 27-years-old. For the sake of brevity, here is the last paragraph:

I miss you so much and you don't write to your mother. In a few months you will be married and then we will have even less time to talk. And have you seen your sister-in-law Pari lately? She has gotten very fat. I love you.

....

Grief is a strange storm to experience—you feel a

constant heaviness that weighs you down as if you are drowning, but then there are moments where the light peaks through. You find yourself laughing when these moments sneak in, immediately followed by waves of guilt washing over you for feeling happiness. Grief consumes you and it often feels as though there is no destination as you journey through that storm.

The years after Mumma's passing were some of the darkest of my life. It took me nearly two years to empty her bag that I had packed for her the first night she was admitted to the hospital. Food seemed to lose its flavor —no matter how much I ate, I never felt full nor did I feel like eating more. Alcohol was unable to numb the blinding pain as I attempted to cram a wine bottle into the Mumma-shaped hole in my heart.

Indian children have a very different relationship with their grandparents than most Americans. For me, my grandparents were a second pair of parents that I had the privilege (and, sometimes, pain) of growing up with. Mumma and Dadaji were the heads of the house and lived with us for eight months out of the year. They would spend the other four months either taking us on vacations or visiting India. Like all grandparents, Indian grandparents dote on their grandchildren and shower them with affection—however, they were also our primary disciplinarians and taught us life lessons that I wish I had had the patience to really take in.

For all of Mumma's bigotry, I could never see her as a bad person. Perhaps, like many, I chose to turn a blind eye to the faults of my loved ones—this is especially true for my relationship with Mumma. Despite her close-mindedness, Mumma was also gentle, loving, and charismatic. That's how I remember her. I never got the chance to say it at her funeral, but here it is:

I would always tell Mumma that she was my favorite, but, the truth is, she was much more than that—in the simplest terms, she was the love of my life.

She was the first person I would want to see when I woke up, still groggy from a lack of coffee. She was the last person I would want to talk to before going to bed, curled up on the sofa arm, falling asleep to the ticking of her mechanical valve. She is the reason for every stamp on my passport and every TV show on my Netflix list. She was My Beloved Peaches.

It's going to be a long time before I come to terms with this. I don't believe that she is in a better place, resting in peace —the thought of an afterlife or reincarnation is completely lost on me. I believe in science. I find faith in the facts. So, here is the truth of it:

1. I had 23 years worth of hugs and kisses from Mumma, yet it still doesn't seem like enough.
2. Inside and out, she was the most beautiful and perfect being that ever existed.
3. There is a great comfort in knowing that the best part of me will always reside within her.

2. PATEL ME ABOUT IT

I knew I wasn't a normal kid at the age of five when I went up to my dad and said, "I don't think it's fair."

"What's not?" he asked.

"I don't think it's fair that you got to pick my name but I don't get to pick yours."

"But I have a name. I'm Daddy."

"That's foul," I said, scrunching up my nose in disgust. I wasn't old enough to know the strange sexual connotations associated with Daddy, but I sensed something was off and wanted to steer clear from that. "From now on, your name is Melvin."

"Why?" the newly-knighted Melvin asked me.

"Because you look like a fat brown penguin whose name would be Melvin," I said before nonchalantly skipping away.

It was 12 years later, when I first went to my best friend Elsie's house, that I was confronted with a room full of stuffed animal penguins.

"What is all this?" I asked, wondering why a 17-year-old had about two dozen stuffed penguins in her room.

"These are all my Melvins," Elsie, who didn't know what I called my dad at the time, said.

"Your...what?"

"Every time I find one, I buy it and name it Melvin," Elsie said matter-of-factly.

I stared at Elsie and knew that that moment was fate. We were meant to be.

Aside from the fact that I decided to change my dad's identity into that of an aging Jewish accountant, I grew up with what I considered to be a fairly normal childhood for a first-generation American. My friends often see pictures of me when I was younger and question why there are seven toddlers sitting in a line on the floor of a kitchen with steel plates.

"There aren't enough tables in the dining room to seat 30 people," I would explain. "So the kids sit on the floor of the kitchen because it makes the mess easier to clean up. The oldies and the men eat their dinners and then rotate out so that the women can eat before doing the dishes."

My friends were primarily white (with a couple of Colombians and Filipinos thrown in), so it was normal that I would have to explain some cultural aspects to them that I took for granted as the norm.

When you're a Patel, you are a part of a cult of like-minded cheap individuals who think *JAG* is edgy for TV. Being a Patel is being part of a network that you will never fully be able to disconnect from.

As far back as I can remember, our home has served as a makeshift Airbnb. Despite that my family owned a motel, whenever extended family or even just other Patels came to visit, they would stay at our house instead of staying at the family motel. Our home has had a guest room that has been consistently rotating out relatives on a weekly basis for the last three decades.

When you're a Patel, there is quite *literally* a port in every storm. Even if you don't know the people personally, other Indians will help you out.

Thirty years ago, Melvin and 14 of my uncles piled into a van for a cross country trip. As they were driving through Texas during a particularly bad storm, they tried to find a place to stay. Melvin spotted a motel and the 15 of them went in. The owners were, you guessed it, Indian. There was only one room available in the motel but the couple who owned it opened up their apartment behind the motel to Melvin and my uncles, free of charge. The couple then cooked a traditional Indian meal for all 15 of them.

Melvin loves to tell this story because it proves his theory that nobody beats Indian people when it comes to hospitality. Living at my parents' house, Marco and I would frequently be told that an aunty or uncle was coming to stay with us.

"Who are they?" we would ask.

"Well...the thing is, we don't really know," Melvin would sheepishly say. "We've never met them. One of Dadaji's friend's cousin's sister-in-law and her family."

"How long are they staying?" I would quickly follow up, wanting to know how long I would be inconvenienced for.

"We don't know. We can't ask someone how long they are staying."

Indian people are so nice that they won't even ask their guests for a checkout date, even if they don't know them. I would argue that Indian people are too hospitable. Personally, I plan to make any guests who are planning to come to my house book through Airbnb, thereby ensuring a proper check-in and checkout date, as well as a security deposit for getting rid of any curry aromas that linger after their departure.

....

Growing up, Melvin and my mom were typical Indian parents. Melvin worked at a hotel and spent most of his free time with his African grey parrot, Nilu, which doted on him and terrorized the rest of us. Melvin was not what I would call a "hands-on parent" with me. Melvin never even learned to change a diaper. The first time he watched my brother unsupervised, him and three of my uncles, (all of whom had children), could not figure out how to change a diaper. Their solution was to hold my brother up in the backyard and spray him with a hose until he was clean before putting him in one of their t-shirts.

Meanwhile, my mom was the epitome of hospitality. My mom loved to make trips to my elementary school just to bring me freshly-made samosas and curry that was still warm from the stove. My mom bought all of our clothes from Sears, as she taught us that this was the cool place for both appliances and a pair of jeans.

While my mom and Melvin were constantly checking up on Marco's grades and ensuring that he did his homework, they left me to my own devices. This was primarily due to the fact that I was overweight, hairy, and spent most of my time with my nose stuck in a book.

As a child, I was an introvert. I spent most of my afternoons keeping our 90-pound German Shepherd hostage by holding her around the neck and reading her stories that I had written about my day. When I wasn't with the family dog, I was outside talking to my imaginary friend, Pennywise. I had secretly watched Stephen King's

It without my parents' permission when I was six and had truly been fascinated by the psychopathic clown. I had decided that naming my imaginary friend Pennywise was a nice way to pay tribute to my favorite villain. My parents never questioned why I was talking to myself outside or talking about Pennywise—in retrospect, they should have sent me to therapy at least a decade earlier than they did. It also didn't help that I had very few friends or hobbies outside of reading and writing. Even my pop culture references at that age were dated as I preferred TV Land to Cartoon Network. I started to frequently miss school by pretending that I had a stomach ache so that I could watch reruns of *The Nanny* and *Three's Company*.

On one of the days that I decided to skip school, I was busy feigning my third stomach ache within a week when my mom and Pari came into the room and closed the door. I tried to pass the flush on my face from laughing at Estelle Getty as an oncoming fever.

"Sejal, we need to talk," Pari said in a serious tone.

Great, I thought. *Well, kid, you had a good run. The jig is up.*

"You're feeling this way because you are about to start your period," Pari said.

I was mortified. I was only 10 at the time and I was faking it, but if I blew my cover, I would never be able to stay at home again. I had no choice but to sit there and listen.

"Your period means that you can get pregnant," Pari continued, while my mom just silently nodded next to her. "Now look. Your brother is a guy so he can have sex with as many women as he wants because he can't get pregnant. You, on the other hand, can get pregnant so you can't have sex."

To this day, this was the only sex talk I was ever given in my life (not counting my gynecologist, who always has to judgmentally explain to me at my annual pap smear why she can't write me prescription for morning-after pills in bulk).

I was a perfect straight-A student yet I still felt the need to skip class, mostly because my classmates did not interest me. I found myself being better friends with my teachers and would often be that obnoxious kid trying to participate in grown-up conversations with my aunts and uncles at parties. My mom wasn't involved in the PTA so I wasn't invited to the weekly play dates or sleep-overs that the other girls in my class would have while their moms guzzled Chardonnay by the liter.

I also never expressed any interest towards boys, mostly because I just assumed they were not interested in me. The lack of interest was probably true since even in the second grade, I had a full unibrow, a prominent mustache, braces, and glasses.

Despite my physical shortcomings, I did manage to attract the attention of one boy when I was eight: a Russian exchange student named Alec. Mrs. Brunson had charged me with being Alec's English tutor during free time because it was my strongest subject. Somehow during these hour-long tutoring sessions, Alec had fallen deeply in love with me.

After a few weeks, I noticed Alec was spending more time staring at me instead of the chalkboard. That day, Alec finally mustered up the courage to present me with a jewelry box. Being the good Indian girl that I was, I told him what my mother told me: "I only accept jewelry from my family." I figured my rejection would be enough embarrassment to ward him away for at least a week. Boy, was I wrong.

As soon as the recess bell rang and I stepped out on to the playground, I noticed Alec making a bee-line towards me. That was when I first came across *that* look, that "You're-A-Fertile-Female-Let-Me-Make-You-Mine" look. I'm not sure if it was pure adrenaline or the fact that I was mentally playing R Kelly's "I Believe I Can Fly" for motivation, but I channeled my inner Usain Bolt and ran for it.

For the next 15 minutes, with none of the five supervising teachers intervening, I was chased around the tire swings and jungle gyms by a manic Alec, who was screaming at the top of his lungs, "Let me put necklace on you! I want to take you home to my babushka!"

I went home in tears and sat on the toilet for 30 minutes before calling my mom in. My mom immediately came with a glass of prune juice, assuming that I was constipated as usual. Truthfully, I was creeped out by Alec...but I was also constipated. I blubbered the whole story to my mom between sips of prune juice with my bee-covered Hanes underwear pooled on the floor.

My mom stroked my hair before quietly asking, "You didn't take the necklace, did you?"

"N-n-no," I cried.

"Good, *beta*. You did the right thing. You only take jewelry from your family and then from your husband once you get married."

....

I remained a perfect child well into my teen years. While Marco was busy hotboxing the doghouse, I would stay up until 3:00 AM to finish homework and do some leisurely reading.

I still wasn't interested in dating when I started high school. In any event, I was told the same thing whenever the subject of dating came up: I could date after I got married. Explaining this to my friends was always challenging, mostly because Americans who hear the words "arranged marriage" immediately think of a child bride being wed to a man 20 years older.

The truth is, up until just the last few years, my entire family all had arranged marriages. Most of my grandparents, great aunts, and great uncles had marriages where they met their intended spouses only once or twice before the wedding. In these cases, some of them were actual child brides and many times my relatives disclosed that they did not want to get married but their parents made them. Meanwhile, most of my relatives who are a part of Generation X or younger participated in a more modern version of arranged marriage. This version is what I like to call Arranged Marriage Lite—you're given a list of suitable people that your parents have pre-approved. After that, they help to arrange simple dates, such as going to the movies or getting ice cream. After a couple of these dates, if both parties like one another, they tell their parents, cementing an engagement.

I know arranged marriage sounds extremely unromantic, and that's mostly because it is. However, this is a system that has worked for generations. On the show *Outsourced*, they explain that marriage is like soup: "Love marriage is like hot soup that goes cold over time. Arranged marriage is like cold soup that you slowly heat over time." With the exception of a few relatives, I have found this sentiment to mostly be true. My aunts would often tell me that they did not want to marry their husbands and that it felt like a partnership that was forced on them. They then follow up by telling me that they can't recall exactly when it happened, but somewhere along the way, that partnership turned into them becoming best friends and the loves of each other's lives. It's hard to argue against this point considering how many times I've seen many of them grinding against each other on a dance floor.

There are also practical reasons for arranged marriages. Indians believe that the best way to get to know somebody is to know their family. Since Indian families are so large and actively involved in one another's lives, it's important for them to ensure that a marriage is not just about two people—it's about the family units as a whole. When Americans get married, the marriage is all about the bride and the groom. When Indians get married, the marriage is about everyone except for the bride and the groom—it's about the union of two families coming together.

In any event, as a teenager, while there was a boy here or there that I would find attractive, I was too busy plotting on being a perfect student so that I could escape the state and be away from my parents' clutches.

By the time I did actually get real friends, I was 16 and had chosen to part ways with Pennywise. Living in suburbia, I had absolutely no Indian friends and this was always a point of contention with my parents. Melvin and my mom encouraged my brother and me to reach out to the Indian kids in our grade and make friends. I found it strange to try to get in good with a particular race at school, especially one where most of them were still using backpacks with wheels to run to class between periods.

The first time Lizzy and Lauren came to my house, it was right before the high school's homecoming dance. This was my first time letting my parents meet my real friends, friends that I knew I would have a lifelong connection with. I sat there in my gaudy purple dress from Macy's feeling my stomach acid turn to diarrhea as I nervously awaited their arrival.

When Lizzy and Lauren came in, my mom and Melvin initially acted normal, ooh-ing and ahh-ing at the dresses and taking a bunch of group photos. After that is when things took a turn. As we are all taking turns hugging my mom goodbye, she stopped to put something behind Lauren and Lizzy's ears.

"Mom!" I said, mortified. "What are you doing?"

Lizzy and Lauren were both rubbing behind their ears to find this black powder there. They looked at me in confusion.

"It's just a little something to ward away the evil," my mom said, as if this explained everything. "Now come here, *beta*, I need to do your ear."

"What?!" I yelled, running away. "No, Mom! I told you no weird stuff when my friends are over!"

The next 30 seconds consisted of my mom chasing me around the dining table with her black powdered finger while Lauren and Lizzy looked on in fascination and horror. I finally gave up and let her put the powder behind my ear.

I'm still not sure if it was the powder or the fact that we were just socially inept, but no evil came to us that night unless you count the Denny's Moons Over My Hammy that we consumed post-homecoming.

....

When I was 16, I noticed that something was still

not right with me. I was doing great in school, I had the same best friends that I have to this day, and I genuinely carried myself with the confidence of someone who knew she didn't need make-up—but something was off. I was prone to manic episodes followed by bouts of severe depression. There were times where I would stay up for 48 hours straight, spending the nights coloring and getting lost in my own writing, none of which I would remember the next day. Then there were times where I couldn't get out of bed for days. My parents insisted that it was just part of being a teenager, but even I knew the truth laid in something deeper.

I started to beg my parents to let me see a psychologist and a psychiatrist. I had done my research and knew that I needed a combination of both medicine and cognitive behavioral therapy in order to diagnose and address whatever was going on in my head. I presented them with a list of recommended practitioners within the area. My parents continuously denied my request to get help.

The thing is, Indian people do not talk about mental illness. When I tell my American friends about this time period, I think they often think that my parents were neglectful and not supportive. Unfortunately, mental illness is a taboo in most Asian cultures. In India, mental illness is not acknowledged at all and it's talked about only in hushed tones behind closed doors. It often seems that mental illness is equivocal to admitting weakness, and Indian families are set on showing strength and pride to others.

I knew I wasn't weak, but I also knew I needed help. After a few months of me continuously asking to get help, it was Marco, only 17 at the time, who convinced my parents that I needed help.

"Something isn't right," Marco told them. "This isn't normal and she needs help."

I'm not sure how Marco was the only voice of reason amongst a sea of adults, but to this day he is still my savior in most situations. Marco knew about my family's dark past far more than I did at that age and knew that I needed help. My maternal grandmother committed suicide when I was a baby.

My mom's mother had been described before as an unstable woman who was prone to manic fits of rage. While many of my family members who knew her suspected that something was not mentally right with her, they could not bring themselves to confront her and openly discuss it. When I was two, my grandmother committed suicide.

To this day, this is not something that is openly discussed. Marco, while always high as a kite, understood that there was a family history of mental illness that had gone ignored once before and the consequences had been fatal.

I finally went to see someone and then another and then another. A few someones and a couple of misdiagnoses later, I found the right shrink. When I went into Dr. K's office, the first thing I noticed was that the entire room was dedicated to various fish. There was no incense burning, serene oriental music playing, or motivational posters advocating for mental health—there were just framed portraits of freshwater and saltwater fish. The second thing I noticed was that Dr. K looked exactly like Larry David, the only celebrity I ever wanted to meet. I liked him immediately.

"You look just like Larry David," I said, taking a

seat on the couch.

"Yeah, people tell me that," Dr. K said in a dry voice. "I got stopped at the grocery store because someone wanted a picture with me."

"So," I said, pointing to the framed pictures, "You watch a lot of *River Monsters* or something?"

"Oh yeah, I love that show."

"I just watched an episode the other day. Something about this fish that can swallow a little kid whole. I can't remember the name of the fish but I liked it based on that fact alone."

"Oh! The goonch!" Dr. K exclaimed. "Do you like the goonch?"

"Well, doc, that's a loaded question. I usually wait until the third session to disclose information about goonch preferences."

And so began my ever loving [platonic] relationship with the greatest shrink in the world. Dr. K was able to correctly diagnose me as having bipolar II disorder and worked with me to find medication that I was comfortable with taking. I mostly like Dr. K though because he calls me on (and puts up with) my shit.

I tend to view seeing new shrinks as an awkward form of dating. I would interrogate various therapists and psychiatrists to the point of bringing them to tears. Once I found a shrink that worked for me, I would stick it out with them until I became tired of their endless prattling about self-love and redundant life advice. I would then dump them and enter the dating pool once again.

One time, I was on a second trial date with Rebecca and talking about my views on dating and marriage.

"You know, Sejal," Rebecca told me. "Sometimes

couples take time away from each other and it isn't always a bad thing. When my first husband and I were not seeing eye to eye, we chose to live separately for a while."

I looked Rebecca up and down, realizing that my mouth was already turning into a skeptical frown.

"Uh-huh," I said. "And how did that work out for you?"

Rebecca stared at me, somewhat shocked.

"I mean, you did just say it was your first husband. Things obviously didn't go so well there. What's the story?"

I have an attitude when it comes to dealing with shrinks and if they don't have the balls to call me out then I tend to walk out. I can always acknowledge when I'm wrong, but if nobody points it out, then I tend to continue on with my sociopathic lifestyle.

One day, I told Dr. K that I wanted to switch my meds because my daily wine was not mixing well with it.

"Do you need to have wine every single day?" he asked.

"No," I said after a pause. "But on most days, I require at least two glasses of wine. I like the taste! Plus, it's good for my heart. Heart disease runs in the family."

"Didn't you say your family also has a history of alcoholism?" Dr. K asked me, gazing at me skeptically with his glasses at the tip of his nose.

"Well now you're just getting off topic. We are here to talk about heart disease. It kills 630,000 Americans every year. I will not become a statistic!"

"Alright, Sejal, don't be so hysterical," he said, exasperated. "If you like the taste of wine so much, isn't there an alternative? They make non-alcoholic beer. Do you know if they make non-alcoholic wine?"

"...Yeah. They do make that. It's called grape juice."

"Touché," Dr. K said as he filled out a new prescription.

3. CURRYING FAVOR OVERSEAS

Growing up, most of the families I knew went on Disney Cruises or to summer homes up north for vacation. My family vacations were always a mix of the exotic along with a hidden element of horror.

During the summer of 2011, my brother and I embarked with Mumma and Dadaji on safari in Kenya. While I was excited for the trip itself, I had needed months to mentally prepare for the travel time with Mumma and Dadaji.

Mumma and Dadaji were notoriously bad travelers. Despite traveling to over 30 countries in their lifetime, they always made the first few hours of a vacation seem like a nightmare—they complained too much about the food, they insisted on getting everywhere three hours early, and they were constantly doing a full search for their passport every 10 minutes.

With my grandparents in wheelchairs, the four of us breezed through security in 15 minutes flat. I found this to be a record, but Dadaji was not thrilled and continuously jabbed us with his cane to move faster.

"Are you sure that thing isn't considered a weapon?" I asked the TSA agent in a serious voice. "I'm pretty tan and I'm getting bruises here. I'm just saying, if you have to confiscate it for the safety of other passengers, then I completely understand."

The TSA agent did not take my complaint seriously.

We got to the gate and the flashing sign said, "Please arrive at your gate 35 minutes prior to departure." It was 3.5 hours prior to departure and we were stuck in the international terminal of the Orlando airport. Being stuck at the Orlando International Airport for more than 30 minutes is on par with starving yourself before a date and finding out it's a vegan restaurant when you get there.

During the entire flight, Mumma kept speaking with her headphones on, unaware that she was actually shouting at me the entire time. Dadaji would randomly poke us with his cane and tell us to look at the map on the TV to see how much progress we had made. Marco had an allergic reaction to the pizza served on the airplane, resulting in him breaking out in hives and me laughing maniacally as we landed in Nairobi.

"Next time we travel, we need to just leave Marco at home," I told Mumma.

"No, no," Mumma said in a very serious voice. "We need him. Without him, who will carry the luggage?"

"Good point. Marco! My bags!" I summoned, clapping my hands twice as if he was a butler.

When we got to Nairobi, I slept for two days straight, waking up occasionally to relieve my bladder before going back to my bed. This safari was off to a less than adventurous start.

On day three, I finally emerged from my cave to load my luggage into the van. That morning, we were going to Masai Mara, one of the largest national game reserves in the world. We were traveling there by van, a lovely six hour ride on some of the most vomiting-inducing terrain. Mumma stayed behind in Nairobi as she had been to several safaris already and had lost interest.

Dadaji insisted on sitting in the very back of the van so that he could "keep an eye out," as he repeatedly told us.

"Dadaji, what are you keeping an eye out for?" I asked after a few hours. "There's no wilderness here, we are still two hours away from the reserve!"

"Ahh, but you never know. I will see everything first, just you see."

I turned around to take a look. While Marco and I were being violently thrown around and popping Dramamine as we trekked up the dirt road, Dadaji sat completely straight up, his aviators on, along with a giant safari hat. Dadaji gave me an impish grin as he gave a sideways glance at his cane to make sure it was properly secured. I gave Dadaji a doubtful look as I snapped a picture, right before hitting my head on the roof of the car again.

While Marco listened to music, I was busy writing away on my phone.

"What are you doing?" Marco asked, pulling his headphones out of his ears.

"I'm writing!"

"What are you writing? Nothing has happened yet. The most exotic animal we've seen is a pigeon!"

"I'm writing a list of all the food I want once we get back to America."

"Sejal. It's only been six days since we left."

"What's your point?"

"My point is that your diet reflects who you are. You're like a Ferrari with a Honda Civic engine—great on the outside, but rotting and rusting on the inside."

"Well," I said, amused. "I'm going to take that as a compliment. I just heard that I'm like a Ferrari and I'm great."

"You know," Marco said thoughtfully after a long pause. "Whenever I see a girl eating a lot, all I can think about is what a huge dump she's going to take later."

"Let's not talk anymore until we get there," I responded.

Upon arrival at Masai Mara, I was skeptical when the tour guide informed me that we would be staying in a tent. I don't do tents. I am by nature a very shy person when it comes to going to the bathroom. Despite being from India, I have never been accustomed to squatting to use the bathroom. Whenever I do squat, I somehow end up with three streams of pee, at least one of which gets all over my feet.

"This is great!" Marco exclaimed. "Finally, Sejal, you'll actually have to adjust to being in the wild. With my help, you'll actually gain some useful survival skills."

I shot Marco a dirty look. Marco fancies himself a wilderness man of sorts, despite the fact that he packs six pairs of shoes and five different jeans for a four day trip to Ohio. Nobody in Ohio even owns that much clothing.

To my relief (and Marco's disappointment) the tent was actually a full on glamp, complete with air conditioning, full sized beds, and a private bathroom. I immediately nestled in for another 12-hour nap.

The next morning, we began our 7-day long safari, which consisted of 5:00 AM morning tours followed by 6:00 PM sunset tours.

The first time we saw a stampede, my brother quickly pulled out his camera to take a video. That majestic moment was improved immensely by the fact that my brother and I narrated the scene by quoting *The Lion King*: "Mufasa! Stampede in the Pride Land! Hurry! Simba's down there!"

Over the next few days, we got to see lions, wildebeest, leopards, elephants, ostriches, giraffes, zebras, hippos, crocodiles, and monkeys. However, as the safari trip went on, I noticed that we were becoming increasingly desensitized to the wildlife. Suddenly, seeing wild animals wasn't enough—we wanted to see wild animals being wild.

"If you look to the left, you'll see a pride of lions," the tour guide told us.

"Yeah, that's fine, you can just keep driving," I said, flipping through my magazine. "Or let me know once they start hunting something."

My brother and I took a break between safari trips to go into the village at Masai Mara and we got to see where the local tribesmen lived.

"You see this?" the tribesman asked me, holding up his necklace proudly. "That is the claw of a lion that we hunted."

"Wow, I don't suppose I can purchase one of those from the gift shop, huh?" I joked.

"You like?" he asked. "I give it to you for $100."

I looked at Marco and then looked back at the tribesman with a baffled expression on my face. First off, I would never wear a claw of a lion—it would clash with all of my outfits. Second, this guy had pulled out his iPhone, which was a newer model than mine, to show me a picture of said lion. Clearly, he didn't need the supplemental income.

That night when we got back to the campsite, I

was curled up on the bed while Marco was taking a dump in the bathroom. Thanks to the paper thin "walls," I could hear everything.

"Hey, Sej," Marco called out. "Want to do this *Cosmo* quiz with me?"

"Ew, are you touching my magazine? Either way, no. Just, no."

"Come on," Marco pleaded. "I'm bored in here and it's not like I have my phone to play with."

"Fine."

"Question one: what kind of underwear do men prefer best?" Marco asked as he noisily farted while flipping a page.

"Let me guess: the answer is lace," I said in a pained tone.

"Oh my god, you're right!" Marco exclaimed. "How do you girls just know this stuff?"

"I think we're done here," I said, rolling over to go to bed. It was 7:45 PM.

I woke up around midnight and my nipples were throbbing. About three week before coming to Kenya, I had decided to hang out with Slutz. Slutz called me her boyfriend for most of college since we were always together and perpetually single. She is one of my closest friends because she has a raspy voice that I find incredibly soothing and has the ability to turn any night into a lasting memory. Slutz loves boozing, sleeps around like she's got 48 hours to live, and is honestly one of my favorite people in the world.

After a night of washing down a bottle of tequila and freebasing opium while her cat, Coca, judgmentally stared on, Slutz and I decided it would be a great idea to get my nipples pierced. I vaguely remember going to a seedy tattoo joint and having piercing clamps around my nipples. The next thing I knew, I woke up with two pierced nipples and a world of hurt.

I shuffled to the bathroom in the glamp and quietly closed the door, keeping the lights off so as not to wake anyone up.

It's fine, I told myself in the dark. *Your nipples are just healing. Just put the saline spray on them and it will be fine.*

I reached for my bottle of H2Ocean and sprayed a generous amount on each nipple and the surrounding areola. Within just a few seconds, I screamed bloody murder. Nobody woke up. I frantically clutched my breasts as I turned on the light. My nipples were no longer throbbing—someone had doused them in gasoline and lit a match on them.

I examined the spray and a look of horror crossed my face. Thanks to the darkness and my poor eyesight, I had mistakenly grabbed the bug spray and had soaked my nipples in 90% DEET. I washed my nipples for 20 minutes straight and then went to bed, dehydrated from all of the crying. As I laid there, I thought to myself how ironic it was that nobody had woken up, even with all of noise and the lights. I bit my lower lip and said a silent prayer to God for my nipples.

....

We returned to Nairobi a few days later and we scooped up Mumma to head to Mombasa to enjoy the coast. My brother and I got our own room, but of course there was only one bed.

"You're sleeping on the floor," I immediately said.

Marco was used to this treatment from me and

went to open the doors of the balcony, which overlooked the pool and the ocean.

"Let's go to the bar," I told him. We had been in Kenya for over a week and I hadn't had any alcohol.

While walking to the poolside bar, I noticed that the majority of the other guests were European. Actually, let me rephrase that: all of the other guests were European and we were the only naturally tan people aside from the resort staff.

While Marco ogled the topless women sunbathing, I nudged him in the ribs.

"Look at that," I whispered.

Marco immediately whipped his head around to see the 12-year-old girl walking around topless.

"What the fuck, Sejal," Marco said, averting his gaze.

"Do you see this shit?" I hissed. "No girl that age should be allowed topless anywhere. She's been rubbing suntan oil on her nonexistent boobs for the last five minutes while she's dancing in front of a group of adults! Do these people want their child to be molested or something?"

"Yeah. Let's get out of here."

My brother and I proceeded to the bar the furthest away from the pool. As we were placing the drink order, Mumma and Dadaji sidled up to us out of nowhere.

"Now listen," Dadaji said, leaning in conspiratorially. "You guys can each have one drink per day."

"Isn't the legal drinking age here 18?" I asked. "Besides, Marco is already 21 and I turn 21 in five months."

"No, doesn't matter. One drink per day," Dadaji repeated, holding up his index finger for emphasis.

"Sejal, drink lots of tonic water," Mumma said.

"Why?" I asked.

"It keeps the mosquitoes away," Mumma told me, chugging her plastic cup of tonic water with the same fervor that I reserved for guzzling vodka or ranch.

Mumma started frantically rubbing her arms with more bug repellant. When she was done, she handed the bottle to me. I eyed the bug spray suspiciously—since the nipple-DEET incident, I had decided that a little bit of malaria was nothing but a speed bump.

"I'm good," I said, declining the bug spray she kept shoving at me. "Besides, my vodka tonics are keeping me safe from the mosquitos as long as I have one every half hour."

Over the next hour, I hoarded about five cups of vodka and then proceeded to my room. I was going to read and relax on the balcony while drinking myself into a vodka tonic-induced coma. When I opened the bedroom door, I immediately stopped.

There, on the balcony and edging closer to the room, was a troop of vervet monkeys. Marco had left the balcony doors open, somehow forgetting that we were still in Africa and not in the Maldives.

I promptly screamed and ran out of the room, slamming the door shut behind me. Marco came up with me after I hysterically told him the story. Sure enough, by this time, the troop had departed.

"They're gone, you can relax," Marco told me as he left the room.

I hesitantly made my way to the balcony and inspected the area. All was calm. I opened up my copy of *Red Dragon* and took a sip of my vodka tonic.

After a few minutes, I felt that I was being watched. I lowered my book and squinted in the sunlight at the surrounding trees. Sure enough, the troop had returned. They were glaring at me from the trees. I scampered back in and closed the door in just enough time to see one of the monkeys angrily swat at my vodka tonic, spilling it over the balcony in a magnificent spray of crystal clear liquid.

My lips trembled as I pressed my palm against the glass door and whispered to my cocktail, "I'll never forget you."

....

Traditionally, I'm the one to embarrass us on family vacations—whether it's by accidentally using my mom's vaginal cream as toothpaste or me being too cheeky with a butch TSA agent in France. The latter resulted in the TSA agent announcing to my family that she wanted to do a full body cavity search on me at the age of 15.

I have horrible luck with security. For some reason, security guards always single me out as the suspicious one, even when I am traveling with my entire family. On the way back from Kenya, I had Mumma's carry-on bag and the security guards made me put it through the scanners roughly a dozen times. In addition, they dumped out all of the contents of Mumma's meticulously organized bag at least five times.

"Is there something in particular you are looking for?" I asked, my patience wearing thin.

After over an hour of searching, the security guard confiscated a two inch long spoon that he told me could be used as a weapon and was a serious threat to security.

"A spoon?" I asked Marco and the security guard. "This is why you've been tearing apart a 70-year-old woman's bag for over an hour? A *spoon*? You've got to be fucking kidding me. Is there a supervisor I can speak to?"

The security guard ignored me as he threw the spoon into a nearby trashcan and walked away.

On a previous trip coming back from India, we were catching a connecting flight in Germany when I was stopped to have my bag searched. The security guard threw about 20 pairs of underwear out of the bag and dumped it on the counter.

I went to snatch my unmentionables when the security guard harshly told me, "No touch. Stand over there."

The security guard then pulled out a 40-pack of markers and a giant coloring book. He gave me a suspicious look.

"I get nervous when I fly," I said, managing an awkward smile. "I basically have the mind of a toddler."

The security guard did not laugh at my joke. He then pulled out three plastic bags all filled with leaves.

"What is this?" he asked.

"I don't know," I said puzzled. "Let me assure you, good sir, I am just as confused as you are."

The security guard opened the bag and sniffed it. At this point, Marco and Melvin were staring at me from the other end of security, as they had both breezed through it despite looking like terrorists. Melvin held up his hands and mimed something to me as he looked from the pile of underwear to the bags of leaves. The security guard was sniffing and passing around the bags to the group of guards that were gathering.

"How do you not know what this is?" the security guard demanded.

"I mean, I didn't pack everything in here," I

blurted out. "My mom packed—"

"Somebody else packed your bag?" the security guard said, cutting me off.

"Well, no, not somebody," I said, losing patience. "Just my mom. I don't know what she put in there."

"It's illegal for somebody else to pack your bag."

"Excuse me? How about all these toddlers with their sippy cups running around here? You think they packed their own bags? I'm a minor, too!"

The security guard was not amused with me and Melvin was frantically waving at me to stop talking. The security guard finally decided to throw away the unidentifiable leaves and spices and give me my underwear and carry-on bag back. My dignity was left behind.

Thankfully, five months after Kenya, I was, for once, not the most embarrassing person during the family vacation. Instead, this prize went to Mumma's brother, Aman. Aman had remarried to a British lady, Gigi, after his first wife died. This has resulted in some of my favorite aunts and uncles being born, like my wine-guzzling aunt, Mandy, and my ever-partying uncle, Nadir. Aman and Gigi divorced not long after having their kids.

In December 2011, we embarked on a cruise to Mexico for a reunion with Mumma's side of the family. As I previously noted, Mumma's side of the family is wild. I'm not sure what the weather was like the day Mumma was born, but I suspect that there's a reason the apple fell so far from the tree. It wasn't just windy that day—that apple was picked up by a tsunami wave, carried overseas, and entered another country illegally. Mumma's side of the family loves to booze, swear, and dance, all things that Mumma despised.

While Aman and Gigi at first pretended that

everything was amicable for the sake of the kids and the grandkids, tensions began to rise over the course of the 7-day cruise. By day three, everyone had had enough. It had gotten to the point where the two of them couldn't be in a room together and they were killing everyone's buzz. While I can't be certain, I suspect that their kids had an intervention with Aman and Gigi because they were sick of the constant griping.

At this point, our drinking had taken a turn for the worst. While battling a storm that the ship had gone through, we had all also battled about 10 shots of vodka a piece at night, not including the imbibing that we took part in during the day. Despite it only being three days into the cruise, we all looked like we had aged roughly 15 years from the lack of sleep and the constant intoxication.

At dinner that night, I was at the cousins' table with Marco, Nick, and Nadir's kids, Kai and Rey. As we were sitting there watching the adults at their table, we noticed that Aman and Gigi were being particularly chummy. They were feeding each other bites of their food and making small talks.

While Aman and Gigi pretended that everything was hunky-dory, Kai nudged us.

"What's going on there?" Kai asked.

"I have no idea, but I don't trust it," Nick said, drinking more wine that we had smuggled him since he was still underage. "They're laughing at each other's jokes and smiling."

"Yeah, that's just it," I said. "Their jokes aren't funny."

We all watched as Aman took a big bite of steak and then spit it out in disgust into his napkin.

"Great," I said, draining my wine glass. "This is exactly how I imagined my birthday to be."

"Oh, yeah, it's your birthday," Nick remembered.

"Yeah let's keep that low-key. If everyone gets drunk enough, they'll forget it's my birthday and they won't sing to me."

I hate the happy birthday song. I refuse to sing it at all events. I think it is uncomfortable, terribly written, and has no rhythm. I will give a polite golf clap when someone blows out the candle, but I have always tried to not partake in any part of the song, even for my grandmother's birthdays.

"OH MY GOD!" Kai half yelled and half hissed a few seconds later.

"What?" we all asked.

"She just ate it!" Kai said, wheezing for air.

"What?!" we all repeated.

"Gigi!" Kai exclaimed. "Aman just took that steak he spit out from the napkin, put it on a fork, and fed it to Gigi!"

The five of us whipped our heads around to look on in morbid fascination.

Gigi was chewing thoughtfully and saying, "Oh, yes, it's quite lovely. Would you like to try a bite of my dinner?"

The beef-stained napkin was sitting empty on the table and Aman gave an evil laugh and patted his ex-wife on the back as he knocked back another whiskey.

4. LIMP DICK

The Year of Sejal was more like a year and half after I graduated where I meandered around, worked at a restaurant, and fooled my entire family into going along with it because I claimed that I was studying for my LSATs. There were a series of events that led up to this decision, the biggest of which dealt with my virginity.

I was about to be 22 and I was still a virgin. By Indian standards, this was normal since sex was only for marriage. In fact, the reason an Indian bride's sari is red is to symbolize her hymen (as well as, I'm assuming, to hide any incriminating stains that come as a result of the wedding night—pun intended). However, I was not interested in ever getting married and I knew I wanted to just ditch my v-card with someone meaningless.

I had countlessly tried to get guys to take my virginity with minimal luck. The weird thing is, I knew I was attractive and I was not looking for a relationship, two things that I figured made the perfect recipe for smashing. I was 107 pounds, 5'6" with long legs, and rocking a c-cup—yet, somehow, I still could not find anyone who would have sex with me.

Let me clarify something: I am fully aware of the fact that I could have had sex if I had just walked up to a guy at a bar and offered myself up. However, I tend to think every man I ever meet is a serial killer.

My logic here is not entirely irrational, considering that I did meet a serial killer. When I was 16, I met Sean at Starbucks and we hit it off. Sean and I ended up drinking four coffees and talking for over three hours. I wouldn't say he was gorgeous, but he was white, tall, and had charisma. Sean was into my dark sense of humor and mirrored it back in a way that I found extremely attractive.

When I decided it was time to go home, Sean offered to walk me to my car since it was dark outside. I accepted and as we passed by his car, he told me he had to throw something in his trunk really quick. I don't know if I even responded, I just remember an internal alarm going off and thinking to myself, *Keep a safe distance. This would be a great chance for him to throw you in the trunk.*

I can't even remember what it was that he had to so urgently put into the trunk of the car. This is because as he opened the trunk, my eyes went to the 6-foot machete and the gas mask laying there. My mouth was a perfect O and I felt sick. As Sean turned around, I quickly averted my gaze and pretended that I had seen nothing. We walked the remaining 10 feet to my car in silence.

"So," Sean said, leaning against my door. "When can I see you again? Are you free tomorrow?"

"I have a family thing tomorrow but we can figure it out later," I said, prying my door open.

The truth is, I did have a family gathering the next day, but, even if I didn't, these were definitely circumstances where family time would be preferable over hanging out with this psycho.

"Okay, great," Sean said in an eerily calm voice, not taking his eyes off of me.

I have no actual proof that Sean was a serial killer, but my suspicions were most likely correct if the next day was any indicator. Sean called me 17 times and sent over 40 text messages. The texts started out normal, asking me about my day and when we would be getting together next. However, as I was clearly not interested in engaging in further conversation with this lunatic, I ignored the texts. That's when the texts started getting angry and the phone calls repeatedly came.

Me: Hey I told you I would be with family today.
Sean: So you cannot be bothered to answer even a text from me?
Me: No. I am with my family. Please do not text me anymore.
Sean: You know, this really hurts.
Sean: I cannot believe you are doing this to me.
Sean: Are you going to answer me??!!!!????
Sean: I know what Starbucks you go to.

I never saw Sean again and made it my mission to never step foot in that Starbucks or its surrounding area without a security guard nearby. I have no choice but to conclude that Sean is living in Pensacola now, where he has several women tied up in his basement.

So, given my prior experience, I was not willing to risk losing my virginity to a stranger. Instead, I targeted the guy friends that I already had as well as the ones that lived within a 500 foot radius who I had mutual friends with (incase I went missing). Unfortunately, none of these guys wanted anything to do with me. They were all somehow convinced that if they took my virginity, I would fall in love with them and would be way too clingy. I would like to take this moment to point out that most of these guys were ones my friends had drunkenly slept with and, based on their performance reviews, the chances of me falling in love or even wanting a repeat of the situation were roughly nil.

"I'll have sex with you after you lose your virginity," was the standard answer I got from every guy I approached the topic with.

During my second to last semester in college, I was interning for a U.S Senator and I was still a virgin. It was at this time that I met CB—I didn't learn his name for the longest time and had chosen to refer to him as Cute Boy, or CB for short. Over the course of a few months, I had slowly gotten to know CB. He was studying political silence and wanted to become a lawyer. He was a shy, tall, smart, white guy that worked in the desk space next to me. CB also looked and acted extremely dorky and this was a trait I found adorable.

During election night in 2012, I learned the true perks of working for a U.S. Senator. We first went to an official election night event at a hotel with cocktails and mingling. This was followed by a huge blowout at a bar, which the senator had rented out just for his staff members. There was unlimited top shelf liquor and endless appetizers for us, all courtesy of the taxpayers' hard earned money. I was in Patron and mozzarella stick heaven.

I had brought my friend Luna with me. Luna, while the ultimate homemaker, also loved to drink, dance like Y2K was about to happen, and play matchmaker. The first time I met her, she took two shots of Jameson at the same time like a walrus whose tusks had been replaced by shot glasses. Luna slammed the glasses down and yelled, "Because my middle name is whiskey, bitch!"

I don't think I asked Luna a question but I'm glad

she responded this way because it cemented our friendship. Luna and I, along with our friend Sleeza, had been inseparable for a while and had grown a codependency with one another that my therapist identified as "unhealthy and stunting" to my personal growth. The best part about Luna is that she's pushy and obnoxious, a perfect combination for convincing CB to make a move on me.

My instincts were right, because that night CB finally kissed me. I wanted to smash but I knew in my drunken state that I would need to throw up within the next hour—while I didn't want to remember my first time, I knew I didn't want to projectile vomit during it. So, over the next few days, CB and I texted back and forth until he finally asked me out. The caveat was that it was a day date.

"I don't understand," I told Luna. "I just want to have sex already. Why do we have to go on a date and why during the day?"

"Well, it seems like you like his personality and you think he's cute," Luna pointed out. "Just see where it goes. Maybe he wants to have a relationship."

I was suspicious but I agreed to meet him for a burger downtown. The conversation felt awkward and forced, mostly because I felt wildly uncomfortable being cornered into a date. When CB walked me to the car, the most disgusting moment of my life happened. We were in front of my car and CB leaned in for a kiss. I resisted a bit and he asked me what was wrong.

"This just feels really cheesy and I don't like it," I told him.

"What's so cheesy about this?"

"Well. You're kissing me in the rain. And to make it

worse, there's a rainbow right above us in the sky. This is just really, really gay."

CB laughed and kissed me anyways. This was the first time I felt icky in his presence. It would not be the last.

Over the next few weeks, CB took me on his version of dates, which involved going to fast casual restaurants. CB was a typical broke college kid and I honestly didn't care where he took me—I was more interested in the part where we would get naked. I wouldn't say that I truly fell for CB, but I did have a crush and found him amusing. One night, he even invited me over to his friend's apartment to hang out with his inner circle. His friends were chugging bottles of Southern Comfort and the girls, who were somehow getting drunk off of this, were stripping down to their bras that were obviously from Target. Just one week earlier, I had poured out a glass of Dom Pérignon that I had a 50-year-old give me at a club and claimed it tasted like shit. CB and I were on two totally different levels and this was not good.

Still, I decided to wait out the situation seeing as I had already invested two whole weeks into this. Finally, a few nights later, it was time to smash. After having a few drinks at a party, CB and I went to his dorm room. I was put off by the tiny space but I was tipsy and figured I would never return there after that night. CB turned off the lights to his bedroom as I went in and I remember thinking that it was strange that he insisted on having sex in the dark.

What happened next is the reason that I quote Regina George from *Mean Girls* every time people ask for the love story of me and my husband: *I was half a virgin when I met him.* I wouldn't call what we did penetration—it was more along the lines of smashing, except it was *literally* that. CB could not maintain an erection and I was growing increasingly frustrated at his attempts. I tried to orally fix the problem but CB would not let me anywhere near his penis. In fact, anytime I tried to go near it, he swiftly swatted my hand or mouth away. After 30 minutes of this, I was fed up, mostly because at this point, it was like trying to fit a piece of cooked spaghetti through a keyhole. My penis fly trap did not want to snatch [pun intended] this up.

"I'm sorry," CB said after, as we both awkwardly just sat there. "I just think I had a lot to drink."

"It's okay," I said.

Spoiler alert: it was not okay. CB had had three beers from a keg, so either he was a lightweight or he really had a problem. I couldn't decide which was worse. Either way, I was trapped there for the night seeing as I had had too much to drink to remember where I had parked my car.

"Also, I'm on Prozac," CB quickly said, right before turning over and going to sleep.

I had a standing appointment with Dr. K the next morning and I quickly filled him in on this latest development.

"Sejal," Dr. K told me. "You know I'm not a therapist. I'm a psychiatrist."

"So?" I asked.

"Well, it's not really my place to give any sort of advice to you."

"Of course it is!" I yelled. "Now, tell me everything you know about Prozac and erectile dysfunction."

The conversation went as expected, with Dr. K pointing out that CB most likely would not be able to get an erection while on Prozac. I wanted to call it quits but I gave CB one more chance in case the first time was just him being nervous. A word of advice: do not ever give people another chance. It was not worth it and my vagina felt offended from the condom full of pulp that had kept mashing against it for 20 minutes. I didn't spend the night.

....

After the incident with CB, I spent some time with my family in Costa Rica for a much needed reset for the sake of my self-esteem. On the first day of winter break, my mom, Melvin, Marco, and I piled into Neel's truck to get to the airport.

Marco and I were severely hungover. Since as far back as I can remember, we had a tradition of getting annihilated and staying up all night before any flight. This makes us the ideal travel partners because we don't bother anyone and simply sleep for up to 16 hours at a time. I could always hold my own and would wait, drunk and packed to go, for the rest of my family to be ready.

Marco, on the other hand, was the reason that Melvin's blood pressure was always at an all time high when we were boarding. That entire morning, Marco moved at a glacial pace as he packed last minute. Melvin kept slamming doors and was vigorously tapping at his watch every couple of seconds—if he wasn't so brown, he would have been beet red at that point.

Meanwhile, I sat by the front door and examined mom's outfit as Neel's truck pulled up.

"Mom," I called. "What is this outfit?"

"What?" she asked, examining herself. "It's a casual travel outfit."

My mom was wearing thermal underwear along with a turtleneck. On her head, she had on a cowboy hat. In her hand, she was holding a beach towel that she planned to use as a blanket.

"Mom, we live in a post 9/11 world. You can't go to the airport like that."

"Why not?"

"Because you look suspicious. You're brown, you are traveling to Central America, and *that's* the outfit you went with? I can't tell if you're getting ready to go to the rodeo, the beach, or going skiing. Pick a theme!"

My mom did not pick a theme and insisted that we start taking the bags outside as Melvin continued to loudly curse the day that Marco was born.

We hadn't even made it to the front gate of our neighborhood when Marco began rummaging around on the floor of the truck.

"Did you bring any water?" Marco asked, panting like a sickly dog at the pound that knew euthanasia was right around the corner.

"No," I told him with a look of disgust on my face. "We're headed to the airport, they would just make us dump it. Also, I have a bladder the size of a walnut."

Marco finally found a water bottle on the floor of the truck. He proceeded to chug it for a solid 10 seconds before suddenly stopping and a look of horror crossing his face.

"What's wrong?" I asked.

Marco immediately opened his door and started to spit before profusely vomiting. Neel came to a screeching stop as I took the bottle of water and gave it a sniff.

"This isn't water. This is gin."

"Oh!" Neel exclaimed. "That's mine. Leftover from a guy's night. Sorry, Marco."

After Marco emptied the contents of his stomach from the last 12 hours, we started moving again. We arrived at Miami International Airport to meet Pari, her husband Viral, and Nick before boarding the three hour flight and landing in Costa Rica.

I had spent the majority of the flight contemplating my own existence. Every time I thought of CB, I would visibly cringe. I wasn't even sure what to tell my friends because I couldn't make heads or tails of what we did. I knew that there was no way those two incidents were what actual sex was like. It just seemed like such a shame. Somebody who was as tall, cute, and smart as him was also completely impotent at the age of 22. I knew I couldn't face myself to try to have sex again because his moves (or lack thereof) in the bedroom were atrocious. At the very least, given his erectile dysfunction, I thought he would try to make up for it in other ways. CB, as it turned out, was not a cunninglingus savant—he basically licked my vulva like a dog laps up water.

Despite never having sex and my experience being limited to third base, I still felt that sex was the most important part of a relationship. A good Indian girl doesn't so much as kiss, let alone have sex, until she is married. With the millennial generation of Indian children being raised in America, this has completely changed. There were no more good Indian girls or guys. Every Indian kid that I grew up with was actively having sex and hiding it from their parents. On Saturdays, they would have sex, and on Sundays, they would have *shiro*.

While my family never talked about sex, they found subtle ways around it, such as telling me when I was 15 that it's important to save all of my "firsts" for my husband once we are married.

"I don't know," I told them. "I mean, aren't you supposed to take the car for a test drive before you purchase it?"

I had already test drove CB and had decided that that lemon needed to be returned to the dealership.

I made a decision right then and there to not think about CB during the next week.

This turned out to be easier than expected, as my family had a week-long of hiking, kayaking, and ziplining planned. On most vacations, my family enjoys sitting by the pool and drinking until dinner time. This time, they decided to go the adventurous route. A note: my family is not athletically inclined in any way.

When we got on the kayaks, Viral couldn't figure out how to make his move. While my mom and Pari watched from a nearby boat, Viral somehow rowed the kayak backwards and into another touring boat. Viral then proceeded to get stuck for the next 15 minutes until enough people leaned out of the tourist boat to help straighten out his kayak. When Viral did catch up to us, he was red in the face and stretching out his legs. Viral had decided to stop paddling and let my 12-year-old cousin, who was sitting in the back, do all of the heavy lifting.

Ziplining was not at all a more graceful affair. Our ziplining instructor, Jose, had taken us to his farm in the mountains to have some breakfast while he went over the safety protocol.

Jose was a beautiful Costa Rican god of a man. He was tan and had medium-sized pythons for arms. Jose's smile made me pee a little bit and his hair was just long enough to have something to grab and pull on. It was my 22nd birthday and all I could think of was all of the dirty things I wanted to do with him. Jose was proof that there were other fish in the sea—except the other fish were anchovies and Jose was a bluefin tuna.

While Jose explained how to clip on the harness, his tiny chihuahua kept crying and jumping up Marco's leg.

"What the hell is with that thing?" I asked. I love dogs more than life itself but I could not figure out why this mutt was so in love with my brother.

"I don't know but this is getting weird," Marco said, shaking the dog off as it climbed up his knee.

"Marco," Neel said, walking up behind him. "What's in your pocket?"

It's at this moment that Marco pulled out three strips of bacon from his pocket. Marco, ever the doomsday prepper, is convinced that at any given point he will starve to death. This was the second time that Marco had been caught with bacon in his pockets during this trip. Instead of giving the chihuahua any bacon, Marco gobbled it down and then went on to grab a few more fresh strips from the breakfast buffet for his pocket stash.

Once we were in the mountains, I went first on the zipline. For someone who is extremely ungraceful, I navigated the first course with ease. My mom followed after. My mom is terrified of heights, water, and reptiles. Given that all three of these aforementioned items dwell in Costa Rica, my mom was in hell. As my mom made her way down the zipline, her scream was so loud that dozens of birds and monkeys could be seen evacuating the surrounding area. By the time she made it down to meet me, I was the only other living organism in sight. Viral, meanwhile, got stuck on the course multiple times and had to have Jose come over to wrap his arms around him and tow him back to safety.

After a few days of adventure, Pari decided it was time to relax. Pari called masseurs to come to the villa and treat us to a spa day. Since there were only three masseurs, we all took turns lounging by the pool and getting a massage. When Nick returned, he hopped into the pool.

"Man, that felt so good," Nick said. "I really needed my glutes worked on."

"Glutes?" Pari and my mom asked in unison.

"Yeah. My butt."

"How did she touch your butt?" Pari barked.

"What do you mean? It was a massage," Nick said, defensively.

"So, you get naked for your massages?"

"Yeah," I interjected. "Are you guys getting massages with your clothes on?"

"Why would we take our clothes off?" my mom asked, genuinely puzzled.

There was an awkward pause as I took in the fact that my aunt and mom had been getting massages their entire lives with jeans still on.

"But, you know, I wonder," Pari said after awhile. "You're naked during the massage. Doesn't your *kakadi* become hard?"

Nick and I both stared at Pari and her sixth margarita while choking back vomit. Pari had just asked her son if his *cucumber* got hard while getting a massage.

"What the hell?" Nick yelled. "No! It's a massage! Jesus."

Nick went to go pour himself another drink and Pari just shrugged.

"I was just asking!" she yelled. "There's nothing weird about that!"

To this day, I have not eaten another cucumber.

....

I had decided that it was best to cut things off with CB after returning from Costa Rica. I had planned on just letting everything fizzle as we had both been out of town with family for the last two weeks. However, my first day back on campus, CB texted me and insisted on me coming over that night. I told CB that I was too busy and had had a rough day already. CB continued to press me until I reluctantly agreed to meet him by the quad after my class.

When I got there, CB looked flustered and I felt nauseous.

"So, look," CB started slowly, wiping the sweat from his forehead. "I don't really know how to say this, but I don't think we should be together anymore."

"You're breaking up with me?" I asked, confused.

"Yeah. I'm so sorry."

"Why?" I asked.

"Well, you know, Sejal, sometimes the heart just wants what the heart wants," CB said, with a zen look on his face and sweat continuing to pour down his neck. "It's nothing personal, but sometimes—"

"No," I cut him off. "I mean, why are you breaking up with me? We're not together."

CB looked stumped for a moment as his giant head tried to comprehend what I had just said. After a moment, he finally broke the silence. "I just mean, I don't think it's best if we continue to be romantically involved."

"Romantic?" I spat. "You took me to Pei Wei."

"Wait. So you're okay with this?"

"Okay with what? We're not dating. In fact, I wouldn't even call any of the outings we've been on an actual date. This entire conversation is unnecessary."

"Wow," CB said, looking relieved. "Thank you. I never expected a girl to be so cool about this."

The conversation from there ended with him giving me an awkward hug and asking if we could still be friends. I told him absolutely not and sent him on his way.

As I stood there in the quad, I looked up and realized that we had been standing underneath the American flag. It's my firm belief that you should never deliver any bad news while standing underneath the flag—it's just unpatriotic. I quickly Googled the phone number for Homeland Security and contemplated reporting him.

5. THE YEAR OF SEJAL

In May 2013, I was set to graduate with two baccalaureates, one in legal studies and the other in English. My parents and grandparents were over the moon, as they had high hopes that I would become a lawyer. I had decided on a whim that I wanted to be a lawyer two years prior and had decided to add legal studies as a second major. I suspect my family was secretly thrilled by this—while I had always been a strong writer, they were more interested in having a lawyer in the family and getting free legal advice.

As my final semester was coming to a close, I began to have an existential crisis. I realized that I had already spent an exorbitant amount of my parents' money on tuition and their hopes were for me to become a lawyer. While I enjoyed law, I didn't feel that I was particularly smart enough nor did I have the drive to go to law school. Nonetheless, I went to take the LSATs.

The morning of the exam, I got to the campus an extra two hours early. I felt confident and collected as I had popped two Adderalls back to back. I took a deep breath and said to myself, "Girl. You've got this," right as I took a step down from the garage exit and fell down a flight of stairs.

I landed disheveled on the floor and looked around confused. Several guys were standing nearby. One of them came up and offered a hand.

"Are you okay?" he asked.

"Yeah, man," I said, quickly pulling myself up and declining his hand. "I'm totally cool. Easy, breezy, beautiful, stress-free Sejal."

The guy looked at me, slightly perturbed, and then proceeded to sprint away.

"What's his deal?" I said out loud to myself.

I then realized that several other people were staring at me too. It was only once I caught a look in my reflection in the bathroom mirror that I understood. My hair vaguely resembled a bird's nest. My left eye was twitching and both of my pupils looked like they had just come back from a rave. My arm was scraped and had dry blood matted on the skin and my shirt. I decided that there was no point in trying to fix the mess that was before me seeing as it was summertime in Orlando and the air conditioning was broken in the entire building that the LSATs were being administered.

I took a seat outside of the classroom alongside another 100 or so of the ugliest people I have ever been next to. Now don't get me wrong—I, by no means, was any prize at this point. However, the sordid creatures in front of me looked like they had appeared from out of a cave and were best friends with a troll that made you answer riddles underneath a bridge.

So, I thought to myself. *I guess this is your life if you go to law school. Being stuck next to 100 androgynous creatures from another realm.*

I was starting to feel really discouraged by the time we were called into the classroom. I felt a cramp in my stomach and chalked it up to nerves as I took a seat.

Within 10 minutes of the exam starting, I realized that I was staring at the questions with so much concentration that I forgot to blink. Once I finally blinked, my left contact lens fell out of my eye and right onto the carpet.

A note about me: I am almost completely blind without my contacts or glasses. I know people say this all the time and when they do, I make them try on my glasses. They immediately choke back vomit as they get dizzy, realizing that they have great eyesight and I'll most likely end up needing a seeing-eye dog. I am fairly certain that if there is ever a draft for women, I will be excluded.

My contact had fallen out once before, when my dad and I went to see *Harry Potter and the Goblet of Fire.* My right contact popped out about 30 minutes into the movie and I was forced to keep one hand over it while I watched the rest of the movie with just my left eye. Melvin cackled away and called me Mad-Eye Moody for the rest of the day.

Seeing as this time I couldn't make it through three hours with my left eye covered up, I weighed my options.

I could leave right now, go drink at a bar, and then tell my family that I was subject to racial discrimination after being accused of cheating, I thought to myself. *Or I have to pick up that contact lens, still fail the LSATs, and expose my eye to all of the bacteria that had gathered on the carpet's floor since 1963.*

I finally decided that the $180 I had already paid to take the LSAT would be a waste if I didn't finish the test. I took a deep breath and grabbed the contact off of the floor before smashing it onto my cornea. The contact was dry and covered in dust. My eyes burned as my stomach produced another cringeworthy cramp. I buckled over and tried to conceal the bizarre cat-like noise that originated from my stomach.

When the break time between the sections finally came around, I hightailed it to the bathroom. In retrospect, I should have waited until after everyone else had gone. If the cramping was any indicator, this was not just nerves and this was not going to be pretty.

What happened next was about eight pounds of pure liquid coming out of my butthole. I wasn't sure if I was peeing or pooping at one point. I furiously flushed the toilet in an attempt to mask what was happening, but Vesuvius was erupting in that stall and there was no hiding that.

As the mountain of lava continued to come out of me, I found it ironic that despite the fact that I was born in India, a country known for dysentery, this was how I would die—on a toilet, evacuating my bowels, in a first world country.

After nearly 15 minutes, I emerged from the bathroom with sweat dripping down my face and a pool underneath each armpit. I made eye contact with two of the brave souls who had chosen to wait for the stall—upon seeing my bedraggled state, both of the girls ran out of the bathroom, deciding that UTIs were better than going into that stall.

"Kid," I said, panting to myself as I pointed at my reflection in the mirror. "You gotta get out of the country. *Fast.*"

....

After a lot of back and forth with my parents, I had convinced them to send me to Thailand for a summer-long internship at a legal aid society. I figured this was the perfect way to kick off the Year of Sejal and convince my parents that my LSAT score of 130 could be overlooked if I had a strong résumé.

This was my first solo trip internationally and I was fully prepared. Melvin was not. He took me to the airport and somehow convinced security that I, at the age of 22, needed a chaperone with me all the way to the gate. I'm not sure who the TSA agent was that made the call to let a 45-year-old man with a Middle Eastern name go to an airport gate without a passport—however, I like to think that this man no longer has a job.

As per usual, Melvin and I were through security and at the gate over three hours before my flight took off. I insisted we go to Chili's as that is the coolest place to go in the Orlando International Airport. I ordered some fruity vodka bullshit and Melvin got a beer.

"Now, Sejal," Melvin said, leaning in secretively. "You know, while you're there, do not talk to strangers."

"That's really not original advice. I expect better from you."

"This is serious," Melvin told me as his eyebrows furrowed. "In other countries, there are a lot of sick people and they'll be able to take advantage of how naive you are if you give them the chance. They'll swindle you for money or drug you or rape you."

I frowned. Melvin had always thought of me as naive which had been extremely annoying for me, seeing as I was skeptical of everyone and everything. Even when my parents would make me my favorite dinner, my first question was usually, "Why? What's your motive?"

"Melvin, relax. I'm already arriving at the clinic two weeks later than the rest of the interns—I'm sure they'll fill me in on all of the necessary survival skills. Also, if I didn't accept a date from the gas station guy who tried to bribe me with a quarter, then I don't think I am likely to fall for anything that Thailand can throw my way."

When I boarded the plane a few hours later, Melvin saw me off with tears in his eyes. I felt only slightly guilty (because I was grinning ear to ear with excitement) but I quickly squashed that when I remembered that he had called me naive.

I arrived in Thailand four plane rides and roughly 36 hours later. After first utilizing Google Translate, I grabbed a songthaew, the red trucks that act as taxis in Thailand. I arrived at LAC, the legal aid clinic where I was going to be staying for the next two months, and was immediately greeted by Damon.

"Hi!" he said, in a tone that was way too excited for greeting someone who had just flown across eight time zones. "I'm Damon! I heard you're from Florida, too! I'm so excited you're here!"

I decided right then and there that I did not like Damon. I have an unfortunate personality where I tend to be intrusive and overly familiar when I meet someone new. This is my way of peacocking and seeing if anyone bites—I figure it's best to reveal my obnoxious personality upfront so that way I don't waste anyone's time. However, when someone else is weirdly over familiar with me, I completely shut down and take it as a sign that they must have something mentally wrong with them. With Damon, I was immediately suspicious.

"So," Damon continued, obviously not picking up

on the fact that me not speaking was an indicator that I was not sharing his enthusiasm. "We're all about to head to the office! Do you want to come?"

"No. No, I do not."

"Oh, yeah, you must be tired! Let me show you to your room!"

Damon showed me the room that I would be staying in as he explained that part of the experience was having a roommate who did not speak the same language as me. Damon told me that my roommate was from Laos and would be moving in the next week. Damon also explained that she did not speak any English.

"Well, that's too bad, I'm fluent in Lao," I told him.

"Really?" he asked, suddenly interested.

"No," I barked, as I slammed the bedroom door shut in his face. I promptly went to my bed, passing out for a full 22 hours before waking up the next day.

The next morning, I proceeded to walk to the LAC office right down the road with the rest of the interns. This is when I met Kim and Russ. Kim was a tall, slender goddess that had just been dumped her first morning in Thailand by her boyfriend back home. Russ was walking proof that not all men from Australia are tan supermodels.

"Alright, so what you do is this," Russ said when we got to the LAC office. "To clock in, just take your name tag from here and move it over."

I watched Russ move a piece of paper on velcro from one side of the board that said OUT to the other side of the board that said IN.

"This is some sophisticated system they've got," I noted. "So. What do we do here? There's a disturbing lack of supervision."

Since arriving at LAC, I had not met a single supervisor and the only directions I was given were from other interns. I started to question whether any of this was actually real.

"Well, we don't really know," Russ told me as he put his backpack on the floor. "Mark and I are supposed to be working on a budget."

"I'm supposed to be working on a funding proposal," Kim chimed in.

"Yeah, see," Russ said, laying down on the floor and resting his head on the backpack. "We all have assignments but they don't check up on us or give us much direction, so we all just kind of move things around on a spreadsheet until someone shows up."

"Has anyone shown up?" I asked.

"Not in the two weeks that we have been here," Russ mumbled as he closed his eyes and settled in for his 9:00 AM nap.

....

Over the first few weeks, I continued to meander around with my fellow LAC interns and pretended that I was doing god's work. The truth is, none of us had any idea what we were doing. For the most part, we spent our days working on presentations for grant proposals, something that none of us had any experience in. We spent our nights going to the night markets to sample street food, buying unnecessary souvenirs, and drinking every bit of alcohol we came in contact with.

Within just the first three weeks, I had already found new ways to embarrass myself.

Kim, Russ, myself, and a few of the other interns would go to the local temple to give English lessons to men and women in the village on the weekends. This was our favorite part of the week. The people were so welcoming and grateful. We would struggle through an awkward lesson of trying to teach parts of the human anatomy to a room full of women and monks, and after the lesson they would load our plates up a mile high with the best Thai food I have had to date. On one of these days, I accidentally walked into the monk's quarters, an area that is restricted to everyone. As I turned the corner and realized where I was, I saw a monk fully disrobing. I got a full frontal view of exactly what he was meditating to every night. That's when we made eye contact and I quickly ran out before the authorities were called for a brown pervert being on the loose.

On another occasion, when we all went to get massages, I had somehow misinterpreted the masseur's questions, resulting in her thinking that Russ and I wanted a side-by-side couples massage. Traditional Thai massages are meant to be painful and leave you with bruises. The next day, however, you feel like you have gone to the gym and have been shopping at Whole Foods your entire life. The masseurs twist your body into shapes that it is not supposed to go in unless you are employed by YouPorn. This made the side-by-side couples massage extremely awkward. Russ and I were in the same room with a thin curtain between us had already stripped down to nothing but a sheer sheet covering my nether regions. When the masseurs came in, they parted the curtains and proceeded to administer the massages. There is nothing more awkward than having your body twisted into bizarre positions in front of somebody that you just met but still have to spend the next six weeks with.

Then there was the time I got attacked by a pack of soi dogs. Sois are basically side streets in Thailand. Before coming to intern for LAC, I had to sign a separate waiver that stated I would not sue the organization in the event that I contracted rabies from a stray dog. Soi dogs are rampant in Thailand and are known to be extremely territorial towards anybody that they do not recognize.

One of the nights after doing some heavy duty shopping at the night market, I was headed back to my room with Kim. LAC had a new group of interns coming to visit and they didn't have room for me to stay there during that week. LAC put me up at a nearby hotel about five minutes away from their headquarters to make room for the new interns. Kim was still at the headquarters but at this point we were codependent on one another...and wine.

Kim and I had to go on a trip to teach a workshop the next day in Phayao. We were both ecstatic as the other half of the interns had just returned from there and had described the amazing hotel and the fancy restaurant that they had gone to.

The last few weeks had consisted of sharing outdoor showers with 10 other people. I had learned to wake up early and to always take the shower with a huntsman or wolf spider lurking in the stall—the spiders wouldn't come near us but they kept the mosquitoes away. Unless you have had a mosquito bite directly on your labia, I am convinced that you don't know what true pain is. Meanwhile, we all shared bunk beds in cramped rooms and had one communal fridge outdoors in which Damon would hoard expired food in and refused to help clean it out. I felt like I was living in the freshman dorm room that I had never had the displeasure of living in during my college years. We were desperately in need of some pampering.

That night, I walked Kim back to LAC. The neighborhood was littered with soi dogs and Kim was deathly afraid of all dogs since she had been bitten by one when she was younger. So, I, who loved dogs and couldn't even imagine anything scary, walked Kim back to the LAC headquarters and said goodnight to her.

"Are you sure you're okay walking back by yourself?" Kim asked hesitantly.

"I'm fine," I said, brushing Kim off and waving as I started the walk back.

It was about 11:00 PM in the small neighborhood and there was absolutely nobody in sight. As I started walking, I felt that I was being watched. Looking behind, I saw several soi dogs staring at me, their mouths slightly parted in silent growls. I turned around and kept walking. My arms were heavy with my three bags full of clothes, paintings, and various souvenirs I had accumulated from the night market. I continued to walk at a steady yet nonthreatening pace.

Within another minute, I realized that there was a shadow in front of my own. I turned around and saw roughly 15 soi dogs all growling at me. I remained calm and was about to turn when one of them lunged at me. I decided it was time to assert my dominance.

I have never felt the need to hit a dog, but in that moment I went straight Michael Vick on them. I used my shopping bags and hit the first soi dog across its face, knocking it down, as I made a loud growling noise and attempted to bark at them as a warning. Just then, another two dogs lunged at me and I did what I can only describe as a helicopter movement to swing my souvenir bags like propellers and hit them multiple times. I knew I was no match for 15 dogs so I decided to start running in that split second that they were all stunned.

I was three blocks away from the hotel, running down an empty street, flailing my arms full of bags in the air, all while shrieking at the top of my lungs. The dogs caught up to me within less than 10 seconds. Just as they were about to go in the kill, I heard a beeping and looked up to see a blinding light. Suddenly, a woman on a motorcycle came screeching up and was between me and the dogs. The motorcyclist took off their helmet and revealed to me the most beautiful Thai woman I have ever seen. She shook out her hair in what seemed like slow motion and revved the engine of her motorcycle. She then continued to blare the horn and flash the lights as she waved to me, signaling me to run.

I stared in shock for a few seconds before I finally found it in me to get the fuck out of there. I ran the rest of the way to the hotel, my face streaked with tears as I continued to shake and lay down on my bed.

I immediately FaceTimed Melvin. No matter what situation I am in, I always call Melvin. Melvin talks in an infuriatingly soothing voice, like he's trying to convince someone not to jump off of the Golden Gate Bridge. Even though he was 9,167 miles away, I knew Melvin was the only one who would be able to calm me down as I edged closer and closer to a panic attack.

"Hey, boo boo!" Melvin cheerfully said, before he took in my expression. "What's wrong?"

I regaled Melvin with the events of the evening between heaving sobs.

"I-I-I almost d-died!" I wailed as I buried my face

into my hands.

I was not expecting what came next: Melvin broke out into a fit of hysterical laughter.

"Sej," he said in between catching his breath. "They were just some stray dogs! You were fine!"

"N-no, I'm n-n-not!" I cried even harder.

"I grew up in India. You know how many street dogs have bit me? It's fine, they weren't going to kill you."

"They were growling and lunging at me, Melvin!"

"Okay. So what you're telling me is that they were doing exactly what all dogs do?"

Melvin could not seem to compose himself long enough to get the shit-eating grin off of his face. He continued to cackle like a witch and something in me snapped.

"Listen up, you nincompoop!" I barked. "Your only daughter and the light of your sad, miserable life almost died tonight. Tomorrow, I go on a long bus trip up the rural mountains of northern Thailand and these are your last words to her. Think about that tonight while you're fighting your sleep apnea!"

I promptly hung up and rolled over in an attempt to cry myself to sleep. As I drifted off to sleep, all I could think of was my gorgeous, mysterious motorcyclist of a savior. Given my latest track record with men, I fell asleep wondering if lesbianism was the next foreseeable route for me.

....

Every week that we interned with LAC, we were expected to send in a journal entry to the owners of the legal aid clinic. The journal entries were meant to convey our feelings towards the program and what we learned.

After the trip to Phayao, I sent the following journal entry to my supervisors:

This has been the worst week of my life—I am aware that I have not had a very hard life. The trip to Phayao, in one word, would have to be: abysmal.

The fact that we were not informed of the fact that the 8-hour bus ride would not include any stops for food or restroom breaks should have been disclosed to us earlier. As someone who is prone to UTIs, I felt this was the very least that LAC could do. Furthermore, I was hungover from the night before due to the massive amount of wine I had to drink in order to recover from an attack by a pack of wild dogs. This meant that I had to swallow my own vomit several times during the bus ride, resulting in my breath smelling like an old fish filet sandwich from McDonald's by the end of the trip.

When we arrived in Phayao, we were instructed to leave our bags in a hotel room and head straight to the local "college." Giving a group of uninformed interns five minutes to get ready to teach a lesson after an 8-hour bus ride seems borderline cruel. What was actually cruel is that we had to hike three miles up a hill in 101 degree weather—seeing as we still had not been given anything to eat or drink, I think that this violates some part of The Geneva Convention.

The "college" was just a random tented area where we were expected to teach a lesson that none of us had been given time to prepare. Upon arrival, our lesson plan was thrown out the window, which was perhaps a good thing considering how haphazardly we had thrown it together. The translator told us that he would have to run the show seeing as the students did not speak English and the revised lesson plan was written in Thai. For the following 2.5 hours, we stood there baking in the sun like awkward American props for the class to stare at.

While the previous group of interns went to Phayao and stayed in a luxury hotel, we did not have the same privilege. Instead, we were picked up from the hotel and moved to a cabin in the woods. I use the word cabin loosely as this was more of an assortment of dilapidated logs thrown together. Inside, there were seven beds and approximately 20 species of insects that we were unfamiliar with along with several others that we were familiar with—cockroaches, mosquitoes, lizards, and spiders. There was no air conditioning and the room was at a balmy 97 degrees with 150% humidity. Thankfully, the owners of the cabin had provided one fan which was an exact replica of the handheld ones obese people at Disney use while waiting in line. The communal bathroom with no door was the real treat, as there was a squatting hole on the ground within five feet of the rusty shower faucet.

At this point, being completely famished, we were excited that we would at least be going out to a fancy dinner with the dean of the college, as the previous group had done. Instead, we were served a sticky rice and chicken dish on a banana leaf outdoors. This meal was sadly the best part of the entire trip.

That night, we spent approximately two hours trying to kill all of the bugs within the room so that we could sleep. One of the insects was the size of my hand and flew, buzzing between the beds, until I finally hit it with a book. When I hit the unknown insect, feathers came out of it. We still do not know what it was but we suspect it was going to murder us in our sleep.

Upon waking up in the morning, the translator instructed us that we would be hiking. Despite spraying 100% DEET all over our bodies and bedsheets, we were covered in astronomical welts that left us all looking like victims of a beehive attack. As we ventured on a two-hour hike, we were ex-

cited to see the waterfall that all of the locals had talked about. My good sir, I have been on waterslides as a toddler that were taller than that waterfall.

We returned to our beds that night to find that the sheets were once again covered in bugs. Seeing as we did not have the option of calling a front desk like the other interns, we spent the next two hours once again killing bugs and being eaten alive by mosquitoes.

The next morning, we had less than one hour to get on the bus. The shower faucet trickled out water as slowly as my urethra from the UTI that I had contracted on the bus drive to Phayao. Seeing as there were seven of us sharing the cabin, we were not all able to take showers. I brushed my teeth outside of the cabin with my last bit of potable water. On the bus ride home, I felt completely defeated. I had a rash on my left leg from god knows what and the rest of my body looked like I had contracted chicken pox.

I am not a complainer when it comes to traveling. I have traveled in Asia, Africa, Europe, and South America. I am used to adjusting my expectations for every country that I travel to. However, for the amount of money that we paid for this internship experience, the program could have made this trip optional or, at the very least, given us a disclaimer of what kind of living situation we would be dealing with beforehand. The only thing we were told by your staff was that it would be an enjoyable, relaxing getaway with a bit of an educational experience. Needless to say, this experience was not as advertised.

When we arrived back at LAC headquarters, the group of visiting interns had left. I was instructed that I would need to pack my bags and move back to a newly assigned room. After lugging my bags back to LAC headquarters, I opened my room door to find Damon passed out on my bed, with the sheets covered in blood. I stepped around the stains on the floor and I poked him awake. I informed him that the room was assigned to me and that he was supposed to have cleared it out 24 hours ahead of time. Damon repeatedly told me to come back later. Seeing as I had just suffered through the trip to Phayao, this was completely unacceptable.

As you are well aware, I then threatened Damon to leave and stripped off the blood soaked sheets. It was at this point that he threw a nearby bottle at me. It was clear that Damon was hungover and sustained his injuries while being drunk the previous night. Following this, I got a lovely offer from our intern, Vince, to beat the shit out of Damon. While I politely declined, I do think it's my job to tell you that the reason Damon is such a dick is most likely because he has never had anyone truly beat the shit out him. I've never had the shit kicked out of me and I know for a fact that that's why I'm such a dick.

After approximately 20 minutes of verbal abuse and kicking him, Damon finally left the room in much worse shape than it originally was. Meanwhile, I was left to bleach the entire room while Damon went to his new clean room to sleep off his hangover. The truth is, we all know he only gets to stay on as an intern because his dad is on your board of directors—he makes a point to tell us all constantly. At the end of the day, you all allow his ongoing bad behavior, whether it's hoarding expired milk in the fridge or leaving a room looking like a crime scene.

As of right now, I am contemplating leaving this program early and booking a flight home. I will update you once I speak to my travel agent. Also, do you have a Yelp page? I need to leave a review.

Regards,
Sejal

6. THE DAY I MET LARRY DAVID

I know most people say that the greatest day of their life was when they got married or had their first baby. For me, those things don't even come close to the greatest day of life: February 13, 2014, also known as the day that I met Larry David.

My life post-grad involved me meandering around Orlando in a drunken stupor, free of any job or school. I was enjoying The Year of Sejal in every way possible, imbibing, ingesting, and indulging in all that metropolitan Orlando had to offer. During this time, I also learned several life lessons that I had not expected. I found these lessons to be rude awakenings and strongly urge anyone who is graduating or in their early 20s to read the below three suggestions as a rule of thumb for post-grad life:

1. Do not shake hands with a cop—no matter how cute he is: I was on my way home from work at 1:00 AM on a Thursday. I had on a tight, plunging neckline little black dress and had decided to take Dadaji's Mercedes Benz to work. My family were all in India and when I have the house alone, I drive a car until the gas light comes on and then switch to another one to avoid paying for gas. I drove a 10 year old Toyota Avalon and the Mercedes drove much smoother. Before I knew it, I was speeding across the main street leading to my house and being pulled over.

When I noticed the flashing lights and siren were meant for me, I pulled into an empty CVS parking lot. I was gathering my driver's license when I heard the cop on the bullhorn speaker: "Exit your vehicle slowly." I was extremely confused—I hadn't been pulled over in nearly six years and I had no idea what the protocol was, but I was 99% sure that it wasn't *this*. I slowly got out of my car but I couldn't remember if the officer told me to put my hands up as I exited. Seeing as I was a minority in a predominantly white neighborhood in suburbia, I came out of the car with my hands partially up, like I was trying to raise the roof but didn't quite get there.

As soon as I saw the cop, I was blinded by his sheer beauty—this Ralph Lauren-esque Greek God stared at me intensely and made me quiver at the knees. "Ma'am," he said. "Do you know why I pulled you over?"

"W-w-was I speeding, Officer...McPretty?" I asked, trying to simultaneously read his badge and keep my clitoris from exploding with excitement.

"It's McPetty," the cop said dryly, holding out a hand.

In that moment, I came to the realization that this Adonis wanted to shake my hand—*he was into me!* Brown ladies, listen up: a cop *never* wants to shake your hand when pulling you over—he is *not* into you. Office McPetty immediately took three steps back and reached for his taser, shooting me a confused and threatening look.

"I need your driver's license, Ma'am," he clarified.

I was bummed and slowly reached out my other hand with the driver's license. Officer McPetty instructed me to get back into the car at this point.

After a few minutes, another cop had decided to join in on the party. He had noticed a vehicle parked in the CVS lot that had not been moved in several days. While Office McPetty ran my driver's license, the other cop came over and was super friendly, making small talk and telling me about the days when he would take his grandfather's car out for joyrides. Officer McPetty eventually came over to my window and handed me my driver's license as he asked for my insurance information.

I was in Dadaji's car and he is an extreme hoarder. When I opened his glovebox, piles of paper fell out, including four expired handicap placards. I tried to pick everything up and my hair caught on my wrist bracelet.

As I tried to disentangle myself, Officer McPetty slowly asked, "Ma'am...are you handicapped?"

I snorted like an exasperated mare in heat, my hair still stuck to my wrist bracelet. "Well, Officer...I'm not really sure how to answer that."

After that, Officer McPetty let me off with a warning. I hung the warning citation proudly on my refrigerator and would stare longingly at the name for months on end. In the end, I learned it does not pay to be a minority or exceptionally horny when being pulled over by a police officer.

2. Always at least try to look your best: When you are 22 and run into your former classmate at the Neighborhood Walmart, you do the adult thing and make small talk. There is one exception to this rule: when you run into your former high school class president at 10:00 AM, holding two 1.5 liters of wine.

I had just woken up and decided for some reason to get an early start to the day, which included running to the store to get my weekly wine fill. I wore a pair of sweatpants and an old shirt that I had already been wearing for about five days with no bra. I was at my peak Year of Sejal self, which meant zero makeup, not washing my hair for five days, and routinely feeling the stubble growing on my upper lip.

At this point, I was also eating like a fiend. I was still on my ADHD medication, which meant that I could eat anything that I wanted and would never gain a pound. There were multiple stops at Publix where I would be purchasing a family size pack of Totino's pizza rolls and a large box of taquitos. When the cashiers would raise their eyebrows and say, "Big Friday night plans, I see," I would always just shrug and let them know I had nothing better going. I also frequented Chipotle at least twice a week and would order two burritos each time. Whenever the employees would go to mark the burritos on the foil, I would casually say, "You don't need to mark what kind of meat the burritos have in them. Both of the burritos are for me. I don't care which I eat first, I'm going to eat both of them either way."

So, it was obvious when I strolled into Walmart that I did not care to be judged. *Let them judge me for my tiny mustache*, I valiantly said to myself. *Go ahead and make fun of my bum outfit and my greasy hair. Judge away that I am buying wine at 10:00 AM! I am Sejal, hear me roar!!*

As I sauntered towards the exit door with my combined three liters of wine just for myself, I heard a familiar voice say, "Sejal?"

There, gorgeous, blonde, and dazzling as always, was Lisa, our former high school class president and basically all round perfect girl next door.

"Ohhhhh," I said, recognition washing over my

dull, unwashed, hairy face. "How are you?"

"I'm good!" Lisa said effortlessly. "How are you?"

As she took in my overall appearance and situation, I watched Lisa's expression change from warm to still friendly, but slightly concerned. I decided the only play I had was total honesty.

"Well, you know," I said, shrugging and holding up a giant bottle of wine in each hand, doing a sort of wave for some reason. "So...I'm great, clearly."

Lisa took it in stride and laughed. We chatted for a few more seconds before moving on with our lives and not seeing each other until our 10 year high school reunion. Lisa was and still is a gem, which is why she never brought up my haggard appearance when she saw me again. However, this was a learning moment for me: if you want people to think your life isn't in shambles, then do the adult, WASP-y thing and pull yourself together before venturing out. Also, you don't need to buy three liters of red wine at 10:00 AM on a Wednesday—white wine makes more sense for that hour.

3. Never curl your hair naked: while living my life up post-grad, I attended my job's company Christmas party. We were allowed to bring a guest and as I had no boyfriend, I figured bringing my brother along would be the next logical choice. While everyone else dressed up in slutty red dresses and crop tops, I went for a festive white sweater that had a kitten dressed as a unicorn on the front of it. I also decided to throw on my Yoda Christmas hat, complete with Yoda ears poking out of the sides and the phrase "Mmmm...Merry Christmas You'll Have" on the brim of it. I was ready to party.

By the time we entered the party, I had already drank about one bottle of wine. Normally, this wouldn't be a big deal, but this combined with the 10 Jameson and Ginger doubles that I chugged over the next five hours resulted in me becoming blackout drunk. Marco was my DD and drove me home several hours too late. As he was driving, I kept complaining that I felt sick. I rolled down the window and proceeded to vomit out of it. Turns out I did not throw up outside of the car and only made it halfway out. The remaining vomit seeped down the passenger door and into the crevices of the window.

"Did you just puke in my car?!" Marco yelled, trying to see in the dark while driving.

"Nah, man...it's not what it looks like," I said, waving him away. I figured if I acted casually enough, there was no way he would catch on.

"WHAT DOES IT LOOK LIKE?"

The next morning, with a throbbing headache, I realized I had to work. As I got ready, I saw that *Ironman* was playing on one of the movie channels. I was home alone and turned up the volume. I proceeded to get out my hair curler and begin to make myself "presentable." I always curled my hair topless because I am an extremely sweaty person and like to put my clothes on last while I am getting ready. As I was watching Tony Stark on the big screen and becoming mesmerized by his abs, I suddenly dropped my curling wand. It dipped down and the tip of it hit my thigh before I caught it and screamed in pain. I looked down and realized that there was a dime-sized white spot amidst my brown thigh. I unplugged the curler, slapped on some under-eye cream, and went to my car in tears.

As I went to double check that I had my driver's license, I realized that my credit card, the one Melvin paid for, was missing. I figured it had to be at the bar from the Christmas party. I sent a text letting them know I would be late to work. I limped into the bar and asked for the manager, who gave me my credit card along with a receipt for $12 and a signature that I did not recognize. Seeing as we were given drink tickets for the event, I had no idea why I would even pay for a drink. I decided not to question it and took my credit card.

I went to the bathroom at the bar to check on my thigh. The entire thigh felt like it was on fire. I looked at the wound, which still was completely white. I could see the singed hair follicles and knew that the hair would most likely never grow back. The idea of working on my feet for the next seven hours brought more tears to my eyes. I pulled down my dress and gave myself one last look in the mirror—I decided that I should avoid mirrors for the foreseeable future.

As I hobbled out of the bar, I noticed the same security guard from the night before at the door. He looked exactly like Turk from *Scrubs*. As I hobbled past him, Turk grinned and said, "Mmmm...very drunk you were."

....

During The Year of Sejal, I had decided to get a job as a host at a local restaurant. My parents never made my brother and me work a day in our lives. I had to beg them to let me get a job working at the front desk at a hotel when I was 18, and even then they only gave their approval because the owner of the hotel was Indian. I ended up working at this hotel for several years, until one day the manager had belittled me on the phone so much that Melvin put it on speaker to listen to everything that this woman had to say to me.

"You're quitting," he told me as he hung up the

phone in the middle of the screeching.

Leslie, the manager in question, was upset because I had called out of work after projectile vomiting in my car. During this time, I had been sick with some sort of inexplicable stomach virus that resulted in me standing at 5'6" and weighing only 86 pounds. Leslie was aware of this, as well as the fact that I had just undergone a colonoscopy to determine what the hell was going on after seeing several specialists over the course of a month and a half. After explaining to Leslie that I had vomited on my way to work, she suggested that I still come in.

"But I'm sick," I told her. "Isn't this a health code violation?"

"It's fine," Leslie told me. "You can sleep in one of the rooms on the first floor and we'll have Roberto watch the front desk. He'll wake you up in case there's a guest."

Roberto was our maintenance guy who spoke approximately three words in English. After I told Leslie that this didn't sound sanitary or even legal, she proceeded to lose her shit on me and started to yell about how she was supposed to be on vacation in Miami and that now she would have to come in. I pointed out that this was part of being a front desk manager at a hotel that only had three other employees. This resulted in Leslie losing her cool and Melvin deciding that I could no longer work there.

Following this, I did not have another job until I was 23. I basically mooched off of my parents, who paid for my rent, utilities, gas, groceries, and partying. I was 23 with a credit card that I never had to pay off. I am aware that I lived a very charmed life. Given this information, you would think my parents would have been thrilled when I got a job as a host at an upscale restaurant. Their reaction was completely opposite.

"What about school?" Melvin demanded. "I don't want your grades suffering."

"The grades are already in and this is my final semester," I pointed out. "Also, I got straight A's...again."

"Well, you still have the LSAT. And you're thinking of going to Thailand."

"Right. This job will help to pay for Thailand. Plus, I already bombed the first LSAT. If I take it again, it's not like I can spend 24/7 studying for it."

"*Beta*," my mom said in her most soothing voice. "But you need rest."

Ever since I had been diagnosed with bipolar disorder, my mother had constantly babied me more than usual. She used this voice that sounded like what I would hear at the other end of a suicide prevention hotline. My mom was also convinced that I always needed more rest and that would fix my mentally unstable mind.

After a lot of going back and forth, my parents finally allowed me to keep a part time job. Explaining this to my friends has always been difficult. They would tell me constantly about how lucky I was to have parents that paid for everything and didn't force me to get a job. When we were 16, most of my friends already had jobs working at fast-food joints. When we were 18, all of my friends were told that they had to either move out or start paying rent. This just wasn't what Indian families did. I explained to them that this was part of being Indian —my parents would continue to pay for everything until I graduated college and got married, so that way the only things I had to worry about were my grades while they would find me a suitable husband.

The catch was that I had to do everything they said. While my white friends could stay out past midnight or go to Miami on a random trip, I had to beg for permission and check in with them every hour via text. If a call went unanswered, there would be hell to pay. If there was a family function, I had to go, no matter what plans I had already made. I wasn't allowed to date. There were always strings attached to any deal, but given the debt-free life I'm currently living, I would make this deal again a thousand times over.

....

Working at the restaurant changed my life. I was hesitant to get back into the hospitality industry given my debacle at the hotel. Restaurants are a completely different game. There were no long hours spent reading *Harry Potter* and doing my homework while just waiting for the shift to end.

On my first day at the restaurant, I met a few of the loves of my life. I also met Erik. Yes, Erik, my now husband (I just don't count him on this list because honestly the jury is still out on him). During my first shift, all of the hosts had to wear headsets in order to communicate with the managers.

I immediately fell in love with Daniela because she turned on the headset and said, "Guys. What's the difference between jelly and jam?"

"What?" the managers asked in unison on their microphones.

"I can't jelly my dick into you."

Daniela was extremely proud of this joke and I immediately knew that we were going to get along just fine.

My first interaction with Erik was less than positive. When I first met Erik that day, I noticed a small hole near his bottom lip.

"Oh, do you have your lip pierced?" I asked.

"I used to," Erik snapped, making his signature disgruntled turtle face before walking away in his hot pink button-down. These were his first words to me, his future wife. I mean, the sheer *audacity* of that bitch.

I turned to Franny, who was my trainer at that time, and said, "Sheesh. What's with the attitude from the gay guy in the pink shirt?"

My original plan had been to work at the restaurant until I had enough money for Thailand and then to quit. However, as my departure date began to approach, I realized that I really enjoyed the job and my co-workers. I even started to not actively despise Erik. Daniela got me to download Snapchat for the sole purpose of capturing each other in compromising positions and then drawing dicks in their mouths, hands, etc. This was a game solely played amongst the managers and the host staff. After all, it's not exactly a secret that, at every restaurant, the managers love the host staff more than any other staff members. In this case, such blatant disregard for personal boundaries and sexual harassment policies were only worth risking with the host staff.

Staying at the restaurant ended up being one of the most rewarding experiences for me, and not just because I ended up sleeping with Erik. Working as a host gave me the one (and only) life skill that I had severely lacked: eloquence. I am, as the French call it, one mouthy bitch. My ongoing sass and screeching are on par of that of a once feral cat with no teeth that is now declawed—vicious sounding, but completely incapable of actually causing any harm.

As a host at an upscale restaurant, I had to maintain my cool in situations involving belligerent drunks and entitled snobs. I quickly learned how to channel a customer service voice that was so serene and empathetic that 90% of furious guests would end up apologizing to me by the end of my well-rehearsed monologue. Every single time that a guest would sincerely apologize and thank me for understanding, I would think to myself, *Yes! Suck it, Dr. K! Sejal has got empathy galore! Check me out.* For the record, multiple people have informed me that since I was faking any niceties, this was not, in fact empathy. I don't care, I'm calling it a win.

After coming back from Thailand, I continued on with the charade that I was going to retake my LSATs and the restaurant job was just a way to learn about making money. My parents and grandparents were not thrilled with me working a job that required me to wear short black dresses that showed off my somewhat-ample bosom. Still, they let me keep working in an attempt to teach me about earning your own money. At home, I would pretend to study when I was really watching *The Office* in my room with headphones on. At work, I would diligently be drawing dicks into Erik's mouth as he guzzled a bottle of Acqua Panna.

As I mentioned before, Erik and I did not get off to the best start. I figured he was some flamboyant queen who, for some reason, did not want to be best friends with me. However, the more dicks I drew in his mouth, the more I realized he may not be so terrible. We loved all of the same books and movies, frequently trading DVDs and leather-bound copies with one another. He got me hooked on *Doctor Who* and I taught him who Beyoncé is. Even Daniela, who would later go on to be one of my bridesmaids, got into the nerd fest.

"I'll be back," she said to us in an Arnold Schwarzenegger impersonation, holding her two middle fingers together, with her pinky and index fingers extended outwards.

"What are you doing?" I asked, looking at what I assumed was a botched version of the Vulcan salute.

"It's Yoga! From *Star Trek*."

Erik walked up at this moment and I brought him up to speed.

"Jesus, Daniela," he laughed, his pasty skin turning to a bright pink like his shirt. "You just pissed off three fandoms all in one."

Erik and I continued to collapse in laughter while Daniela just shrugged and walked away. Erik grew on me over time, regardless of what a dick he could be (although, this was probably what attracted me to him, seeing as I am a huge dick myself). One time, the hosts were not filling out their checklists daily. Instead of talking to us like human beings, Erik chose to write a passive aggressive note on the binder that said following:

ATTENTION HOSTS: The checklist must be filled out every day. This is not optional.
THANK YOU,
Management.

I retaliated by sending Erik a link to his work email for a Buzzfeed article entitled "How to Write a Passive Aggressive Letter." I followed this up with a nod to Office Space by leaving this in the body of the email: "Here. If you could read this, that would be great. You're welcome."

Erik never replied to my email and it was a dick move on his part. Still, I continued to feel an attraction to him and I knew it was reciprocated based on the late night conversations we would have for hours via Snapchat. When my grandmother died, Erik was one of the first people I told. He was sympathetic without making me uncomfortable. I hate to admit it, but I actually missed him during those few days.

My grandmother died on Monday and I was back to work that Friday.

"Can't you take some more time off?" my parents pleaded with me.

"Nope. They're slammed and really need me." It was the day after Thanksgiving—no restaurant was slammed in Orlando, but I had to get away from all of my great aunts and their inane, 24-7 squalling.

When I came in, Daniela was at the podium and immediately gave me a pouty face and tried to give me a hug.

"No," I said flatly. "We aren't doing that. I don't want any extra sympathy, I just want things to go back to normal. I need to be distracted."

"Okay," Daniela responded as two guests walked in. "Take these two guests to 402."

As I walked with the menus, I passed by Erik and the new manager-in-training, Mary. Erik just said, "Oh," as I came by and I gave a quick smile and nod.

As much as I wanted distractions on my first day, the biggest distraction was one in which I wanted no part of. A couple came in with their 6-year-old boy. I walked them to a nearby table and made small talk. I placed some menus on the table as this little kid, who had no business being in a nice restaurant, slid underneath the table with his crayons. I walked away without thinking much of the interaction.

A few minutes later, I stepped outside to silently cry and collect myself. I'm not sure what triggered this, but, since the funeral, I was prone to random fits of crying. When I came back in, I saw the lady from the party I had just seated talking to Mary in a concerned manner. As the lady went back to her table, she shot me a scornful look. Erik and I approached Mary.

"Everything okay?" Erik asked, all business.

"Well, uh," Mary started, still looking uncomfortable. "The lady told me that she did not think Sejal's skirt was appropriate and that she wanted to file a complaint with corporate. She said that when they sat down, her son saw her underwear and said, 'Oh, Mommy!' She told me she didn't want to embarrass you by talking to a male manager and that's why she asked to speak to me."

Erik laughed, relieved it wasn't a real complaint, but I was confused.

"Wait," I interjected. "Her son was on the floor of the booth. Of course he could see up my skirt from that angle! Also, the joke is on her, because I'm not even wearing any underwear right now!"

Erik and Mary both laughed. I, on the other hand, was enraged. How dare this lady harass me on my first day back after my grandmother died?!

"Well, if it wasn't your underwear maybe it was... something else?" Erik suggested, still trying to stifle a laugh.

"How dare you? I keep my sausage pocket neatly waxed. It's like a dolphin down there!"

I went on for the next 45 minutes about how this lady was clearly threatened because her Ann Taylor cardigan showed that she gave up trying years ago and her frozen cunt hosting vagcicles was clearly not cutting it for her husband. Also, since they had to bring their child with them on date night, her life clearly sucked. A little over an hour later, as they left, I purposely jutted my leg out of my skirt as I waved to them and said in my most sickeningly sweet customer service voice, "Goodnight. Have a wonderful evening. We hope to see you soon," all while I was holding up my middle finger behind the podium.

....

On Thursday, February 13, 2014, I was standing at the podium with Daniela and Ana when my heart had its first real series of palpitations (to be fair, the ADHD pills I was addicted to may have been a contributing factor). It was 9:45 PM and the restaurant was completely packed. Despite the restaurant closing at 10:30 PM on Thursdays, There was a two hour wait to be seated at one of the cocktail tables and the regular dining room was at a three hour wait. As the front door opened, I looked up and immediately thought I was having a stroke. There was Larry David, walking between two men, casually approaching the podium. My panties immediately became a Sham-Wow for what was coming out of my vagina.

Look, I have spent hours, days even, trying to explain my attraction to Larry David. I cannot explain it, it simply is. Larry David has played an integral part in my life since creating *Seinfeld*. I love that the character of George Costanza is based on Larry David because at the end of the day, he really was the most relatable character. I watched *Curb Your Enthusiasm* from day one and watch at least one episode every day—yes, even now. I think *Clear History* and *Whatever Works* are Oscar-worthy masterpieces. Larry David was so exceptionally attractive to me because almost every single thing he does in shows and movies represents choices that I would most likely make. To this day, he is still the only celebrity that I have ever wanted to meet.

Larry's friend, Maxwell, approached the podium and asked for a table for four.

"Sorry, we're completely booked for the evening," Daniela said flatly.

"The bar is available but there's a two hour wait for the high top tables and we close at 10:30 PM," Ana said in a more angelic voice.

The entire time that these two nincompoops were talking, I was stomping on their feet with my kitten heels.

"Surely there's something that you can do?" Maxwell asked, giving us a giant cheeseball smile.

"No, we are fully booked—" Daniela began.

"NO, WE'RE NOT!" I interrupted, using my height as leverage and forcing my orangutan arms to cover the span of the podium, pushing Daniela and Ana out of the way.

Maxwell stared at me with slight concern in his eyes. "Why are you smiling like that?"

"I'm smiling...I'm smiling...because I AM MEETING LARRY DAVID," I said in my most manic voice, my heart pounding.

"You know him?" Maxwell asked, seeming surprised.

At this point, Larry stopped eyeing the white fish in the meat display and made eye contact with me and gave a small smile and nod.

"OF COURSE I KNOW HIM! I WATCH CURB YOUR ENTHUSIASM EVERY SINGLE DAY!"

"Really?" Larry asked, mildly amused. "What episode did you watch today?"

Larry was trying to test me and he was not prepared for me immediately going on to gush, "The one where Oscar needs to be put down and you and Jeff were supposed to get him Pinkberry, but you two eat all of the Pinkberry first!"

Larry nodded and actually gave me a full smile with a chuckle. I stared on with the biggest smile on my face and said a silent thank you to God for making sure I wore my tightest, most low-cut dress from Nasty Gal.

"You look just like my shrink!" I blurted out. Honestly, this was already a weird thing to say at the moment, but I proceeded to make it even more awkward by pulling out my phone and going to my photos. I showed Larry a picture of Dr. K that I had recently sneaked during one of our sessions to show Erik and a few other people that he in fact did look like Larry David.

"Huh," Larry said, looking at the picture with either concern or amusement.

"So," Maxwell interrupted. "That table?"

"Oh, absolutely," I said, grabbing a few menus. There were only two tables open in the restaurant: the chef's table, which was a private half-crescent booth, and then a regular booth in the dining room. I walked the party over to the chef's table, explaining that they would have privacy but could watch their food be cooked on our wood-fire grill. Maxwell and the other guy seemed fine with it.

"What do you think, Larry?" Maxwell asked.

"It's uh, I don't know," Larry said. "It's uh, no, I don't like it."

"What don't you like about it?" Maxwell asked.

Maxwell seemed impatient, but I for one could not be more thrilled. Larry David on *Curb Your Enthusiasm* is legitimately Larry David in real life—and here I was, getting to see a real life bit that he was performing.

"I don't know, what is this? It's a booth, but a half circle? I don't want to sit next to any of you in an intimate way. What, I'm going to be cutting my fish while turning my neck sideways the whole time to have conversation? My neck will hurt. And, uh, I don't need to see my food being prepared. Who wants to see that?"

"I have a regular booth available if you would like to see that?" I quickly said once the bit was done.

As we walked towards the other booth, several people turned around to see him. One guy held out his hand for a high-five. Larry looked at the man's hand in disgust, as he was clearly in the middle of eating his steak. Larry settled for a nod and a polite wave, from a distance.

As they settled into the booth, Maxwell turned to me and asked if I was Indian.

"Yes. I was born there, actually."

"Wow," Maxwell said, his cheesy voice becoming thicker. "Larry and I were just talking about how beautiful Indian women are the other day. Weren't we, Larry?"

Larry looked up from the menu and gave a "Meh," with an approving nod.

"Isn't she beautiful?" Maxwell asked, gesturing towards me.

"Yes, very pretty," Larry said, politely.

"Your server will be over shortly. Enjoy your meal!" I quickly gushed and walked away.

I went running to Erik, walking slightly awkwardly as my vagina basically felt like Niagara Falls.

Larry David just said that I was pretty!!

"Erik! Larry David is here!" I squealed, handing him the table ticket.

Erik looked at the ticket and then looked up at me, confused. "Wait, your shrink? Or, like, the *real* Larry David?"

"THE REAL LARRY DAVID!"

"Okay," Erik smirked. "Sure."

"I'm serious! Go check!"

Erik rolled his eyes and I watched him lazily walk over to Larry's booth. Erik's smug face made me want to trip him the entire way over there. He returned within 20 seconds.

"Holy shit. It's him!"

"I KNOW!"

For the next hour and a half, I kept coming up with excuses to walk close to Larry's table. I watched as he ordered the whole red snapper and requested that it be prepared grilled and free of any seasoning. There was a Jewish God dining among us and I was ready to convert.

As Larry left that evening, I held the door open for him and said my goodbyes, my heart still pounding. Maxwell had decided to take his sweet time and was chatting up Erik (maybe it was about business or the weather or sports games—I didn't care either way).

"Why didn't you ask for a picture with him?" Daniela asked me as I leaned against the podium, trying to catch my breath.

"No my god. Larry would HATE that. I could never disrespect him by asking for a photo."

For the next few minutes, I watched out of the frosted double doors of the restaurant as several flashes went off. Then I saw the unmistakable shadow of Larry come barging into the restaurant.

"Jesus, what the fuck is taking so long?" he demanded, yelling at Maxwell.

"What?" Maxwell cluelessly asked.

"Pictures! I got people asking for my fucking picture outside. Let's go!"

And on that poignant note, Larry departed from my life. I know I will never see him again, but this was somehow the perfect ending. To this day, this is my only celebrity sighting that is memorable. Every time a new season of *Curb Your Enthusiasm* airs, I wait for an episode about a psychotic host who ends up stalking Larry. If on the off chance you're reading this, Larry, I give you full permission to all rights in this chapter. You're welcome.

7. MONSTER-IN-LAWS AND MELVIN

I find people's meet-cute stories to be extremely dull, so I will go ahead and spare you all of the boring details and skip to the main point: ladies, I am proof that sleeping with your boss does pay off. This is one of the many reasons that our relationship was kept secret from all of our friends and family for the first five months. Once I left the restaurant in May, we began to fabricate a story of our dating timeline for the public eye. I'm not sure why we decided this, since neither one of us are famous or have high-powered careers—we worked in the restaurant industry, everyone was already sleeping with everyone.

By July of that year, I had decided it was time to tell my parents. While I had always had a fairly active social life, especially in my early 20s, constantly lying to them about my whereabouts was getting exhausting. I made up elaborate lies every time I went to see Erik—Slutz had a water leak and needed help cleaning the mess, Lauren needed a babysitter for the night, or, my favorite, I have diarrhea and am too scared to drive home. In retrospect, I probably gave my parents the impression that I had really incompetent friends or that I should see a gastroenterologist (both of which are still true). I love lying and it comes naturally to me (something that Erik has always seen as a "red flag" for some crazy reason). However, after several months of lies, even I was ready for some sense of normalcy.

Since Erik had already told his mom about us, he had been antsy about when I would tell my parents. So, on one muggy July evening, as I was waiting to leave for a friend's birthday, I decided to tell Melvin and my mom. My mom was in the kitchen doing something with curry and Melvin was sitting on the sofa watching Netflix.

"So, guys," I said in my most nonchalant voice, plopping down on the sofa. "There's something I want to tell you."

My mom let out a vague, "Huh," from the kitchen and kept rummaging through the pots and pans. Melvin lowered the volume on the TV and turned towards me with a serious face—he had sensed there was a disturbance in the force.

"I'm seeing someone. His name is Erik. I met him at MoonFish and he's a manager there. I like him and he would love to meet you guys whenever you are ready for it."

You know that saying, a deafening silence? I never truly understood that euphemism until that moment. The silence that followed was louder than anything I had ever heard. While I had spoken those words in a robotic, rambling sort of way, I knew they had heard every word perfectly.

My mom was the one to break the silence with this little gem: "What is he?"

"What do you mean?" I asked in a faux-innocent voice.

"What. Is. HE?" my mom asked again. For the

record, my mom is not a scary person. Her nickname is BB (Bela Ba) and she legitimately has the overall appearance and demeanor of Dobby the House-Elf. However, in this moment, her eyes were bulging out of their sockets and her face had gone stone cold.

"Erik is white, Mom."

My mom went completely quiet and Melvin took over. "How old is he?"

"Erik is 28," I responded, making sure to use his name. I heard on *Dateline* that if you're ever in a situation where you are in danger, you should give away as many personal details as possible and use names in order to humanize yourself—I figured the same rules applied here.

"Isn't that a little old for you?"

"It's a five year difference, Melvin. Aren't like three of my aunts 10 years younger than their husbands?"

Melvin gave a contrite look before asking the most important question for every Indian parent: "Where did he go to college?"

"Erik didn't go to college. He took a few courses but he had to pay his own way through. He ended up liking the hospitality industry and worked his way up to management. You don't need a degree for that."

"Hmm," Melvin grunted, sitting back in his chair with the same terrifying expression. My mom was still frozen in place in the kitchen, holding the same frying pan.

"Alrighty," I awkwardly said, slowly getting up from the sofa.

"Sit down." Melvin is also not a scary person in general. However, when he wants to be, he really pulls out all the guns and his stern tone and frigid demeanor told me that I needed to stay put.

Nobody said anything at this point. Melvin scrolled through Netflix and decided to put it on a documentary about King Henry VIII. To this day, Melvin vehemently denies this. After I pointed out that I have text message proof from July 11, 2014, the day I told them, Melvin tried to say he just put it on the first thing he saw. Now, not to brag, but I have taken two psychology classes, and this definitely speaks to his subconscious. Melvin was clearly trying to show me the repercussions of dating or marrying a white man: you will end up being cheated on and having your head cut off.

Me: Ummm. I need you to get here ASAP. I just told my parents about Erik. And nobody has said anything in over 30 minutes. Now Melvin has put on a documentary about King Henry VIII.
Daniela: Okay. Be there soon, friend.

I sent this text to Daniela, as her and her boyfriend were supposed to be picking me up for the birthday party at a nearby tequila bar. I sat there in painful silence with my parents for another 20 minutes, until Daniela rang the doorbell. Daniela is well-versed in awkward scenarios. She knew that my parents would not handle the fact that I was dating a white guy well and she felt ready to be a buffer. Unfortunately for Daniela, feeling ready to be a buffer and actually being prepared are two drastically different things.

Daniela walked in and immediately sat down on a chair. After exchanging pleasantries, she looked from Melvin to my mom and immediately blurted out, "Sooooooo. Did you guys have an arranged marriage or something?"

....

Two weeks after telling my parents, they had agreed to dinner at their place to meet Erik. I had a doctor's appointment that afternoon that involved a stress test. My readings were alarming and I had to explain to the cardiologist that I was simply a bundle of nerves already because my very white, non-college attending boyfriend was about to meet my brown family. The cardiologist gave me a pass on the test and informed me that I needed to stop popping ADHD pills. I thanked him and then proceeded to my car, where I promptly opened up an Adderall capsule and rubbed the powder all over my gums. I checked my phone and made sure that Lizzy was on schedule. I had previously informed Lizzy that she would be coming along as a buffer and to meet us at Erik's apartment.

When I got to Erik's apartment, I could hear him retching in the bathroom, promptly followed by a flush. Erik emerged from the bathroom looking the color of Colgate toothpaste with sweat beaded on his forehead. The stains on his underarms resembled the result of an inflatable pool tipping over.

"Uh...everything okay?"

"I think I'm just nervous."

"Roger that. I'm going to get changed. Then let's have a drink to calm our nerves. You can't look like this when you meet them."

Erik and I proceeded to have a drink on the balcony while I looked approvingly at the bottle of Decoy wine that he had gotten for Melvin and the flower bouquet he had gotten for my mom. Two shots of Jameson and a couple of beers later, as we were both feeling slightly more at ease, Lizzy showed up. I instructed Lizzy to get in my car. My parents were under the impression that I was staying at Lizzy's house several nights a week to make for an easier commute to the law office I was working at. I really needed to sell the lie.

As Erik followed my beat up Toyota, I came to a halt at a stop sign. As I inched up to get a better view of the street, I heard a loud bang and my car was pushed up by two feet.

"What the fuck? Did Erik just rear-end me?"

"I feel like there's a joke in there somewhere," Lizzy pondered.

"Not the time!" I snapped, pushing my car door open.

Erik got out of his car with a sheepish expression on his face and shrugged. "Oops."

"Dude. What the fuck," I repeated.

"I thought you were going!"

"So....you decided to gun it? Tighten up! We haven't even gotten to the hard part yet."

In retrospect, this was not the right thing to say. I tend to have very inappropriate reactions to people's emotions on a daily basis and today was not going to be the day that I made an exception. While my parents were not actively hateful people, they did have certain racist tendencies. For example, my parents have friends of every race. In fact, Melvin has several half-white cousins that he grew up with and loves dearly. However, when it was his daughter dating someone who was not Indian, it always came down to corruption. To them, anyone who was not Indian was an imminent threat to our family—in their minds, there was no way that a white guy with no college education could understand their values and culture.

The dinner that followed was uncomfortable for

so many reasons and I cannot figure out which was the worst: my mom (a recovering alcoholic) trying to pour a beer in secret in the kitchen, resulting in me wrestling it out her hands and spilling a Coors Light all over my dress; Melvin unable to control his glaring at Erik while he just tried to talk about the weather; Lizzy being super chipper and bantering with nobody playing along; or perhaps it was the million silences during the dinner that were followed by my parents doing the signature Indian head bobble.

The next day, we had a birthday celebration for Pari and Viral at a restaurant. During this time, Neel asked what was new with me and if there were any boyfriends that he should be aware of. I was all for transparency, but the minute that I went to open my mouth, Melvin and my mom gave me the death stare.

The months that followed were not much better. My mom and Melvin kept changing their strategy. One minute they would ask if I was serious about Erik and, if so, why had we not discussed marriage yet (keep in mind we had been dating for less than one year). The next minute, my parents would tell me that I need to dump Erik because he was the reason I was not in law school. Melvin was also catching on to the fact that I was not in fact staying at Lizzy's several nights a week. Around October, Melvin told Marco his theory and my brother decided that the best response would be to openly laugh in his face.

"Hahahahahahahahah. Of *course* she's not at Lizzy's!"

"This is serious. You don't know what they're doing."

"We *know* what they're doing."

"WHAT?" I wasn't there, but in the recap that Marco gave me, I'm fairly certain Melvin's eyeballs were actually popping out of their sockets.

"Look, Dad, do you really think I would let Sejal date a guy that I didn't approve of? Let's face it, I'm way tougher on everyone than you are. If I approve, so should you."

The rest of the details of this conversation were never well documented in my journals, but all I know is from that day forward, my parents accepted Erik with open arms. Marco has always been my biggest champion (and critic) and I am convinced that it is solely because of him that my parents finally came around to seeing Erik as a person instead of just a bubbled-in mark under "Caucasian" on a census form.

My parents' acceptance of Erik was the first hurdle. The second one was Dadaji. He flew back from India the night of our annual Diwali party at my aunt's house. Dadaji had already said that he would be too tired from his travels to attend the party but that he wanted to meet Erik. This was the first family function where Erik was joining us and while I was nervous about that, I was more nervous about our patriarch, Dadaji, meeting my slightly older, super white boyfriend.

As it turns out, I had no reason to worry. Dadaji could not have been more warm and welcoming towards Erik. He made small talk despite that he was severely jet lagged and gave a genuine smile whenever Erik would speak. While Mumma and Dadaji had always been low-key racist, Dadaji acted like race was the last thing on his mind. This was almost one year to the date that Mumma had passed away and I think her death truly mellowed Dadaji in ways that even we couldn't have predicted.

When we arrived at the Diwali party, Pari immediately introduced herself to Erik. Pari has always been one of my most open-minded family members and was over the moon that I was finally dating someone. She was several gin and tonics deep at this point and proceeded to pull me aside to not-so-quietly say, "So…how is the sex?"

While I was pleased that Pari's idea of a sex talk had changed since I was a child, I was also mortified that she had asked that question. However, I also knew that Pari was not one to drop the subject until she received an answer. I quickly gave Pari a thumbs up before rejoining my mom.

We proceeded to make the usual rounds, saying hello to the various aunties and uncles and touching the feet of the elders. Bowing down to touch the feet of your elders is considered a sign of respect in Hindu culture—I always found it to be more of a form of spreading fungal infections. Each time we would say hello to someone, my mom would stop to introduce Erik in the following manner:

"This is Erik," my mom would say, feeling the need to point to him even though it was so obvious, seeing as he was the only white guy who rode with us. "He's Marco's friend."

"Why are you telling them that Erik is Marco's friend?" I asked after the tenth introduction like this, pulling her aside.

"Well, it just seems easier."

"People are clearly going to think Marco is gay because, all of a sudden, for the first time in 10 years, he's bringing a guy to this family function."

Marco and Erik couldn't help it and laughed, while my mom realized that I was right. From then on, she introduced Erik as "Sejal's friend." Erik asked me why she couldn't just say the word boyfriend.

"Boyfriend and girlfriend are not terms we use," I explained, heading to the indoor bar to grab some drinks. "To Indians, it's akin to using the word *lover*."

Erik made a sour face as I ordered a vodka soda for me and gin and tonic for him.

"Exactly. Nobody wants to hear the word *lover*—it's unseemly! Boyfriends and girlfriends are referred to as friends, even if the whole family knows the implication, until the day that they get engaged. After that, it's all kosher."

"But you don't even want to get married," Erik pointed out, handing me my vodka soda. "So, what, I'll just be your *friend* forever?"

"Yep," I told him, getting ready to take a sip.

"Fine," Erik said, snatching the cocktail out of my hands. "*Naan* for you."

....

Meeting Erik's family was the complete opposite of what Erik had to endure. Erik, being a part of a typical white suburban family, had always been allowed to have girlfriends. Moreover, he was allowed to have girlfriends sleep in the same room as him and even move in with them once he was 18. When we first started dating, I was always jealous about this fact. To be clear, I was never jealous of the myriads of women that Erik had bedded (him being a hussy was one of his main attracting features)—I was jealous of the fact that he was given complete freedom to be an adult and be treated as one since he was 18.

Maybe it's the wisdom of age or just growing more into my parents each day, but, looking back on this, I think it was a huge mistake for Erik (or anyone, really) to be given this kind of freedom at such a young age. Erik has had a series of failed relationships, most of them involving him moving in with a woman within a few months of dating and ending in disaster while being stuck in a lease. There were girlfriends who stole from him and girlfriends who lost their jobs and he got stuck footing the bill for them and their parents. Meanwhile, I had never experienced this kind of detrimental blow to my mental or financial health from a boyfriend. Maybe this was because my parents were very strict about dating or maybe it was because I was still receiving a monthly allowance until the age of 26—who knows, okay?

When I told my parents that I was going to go down to south Florida to meet Erik's family, the first question my mom asked me was how many bedrooms the house had.

"Uh...I don't know. That wasn't really the first question I thought to ask Erik about his mom."

"Well," my mom said, leaning in to whisper to me conspiratorially. "You need to know. Will you have your own bedroom?"

I laughed in her face and then quickly straightened up as she glared at me and shot a look at Melvin, who was cluelessly paying bills in the office. "Erik can sleep on the couch if there aren't enough bedrooms," I lied, seeing as this was during the time when my parents were not Team Erik.

The entire drive down I was a nervous wreck. Erik's mother, Ma, was extremely easy-going from what Erik had told me. However, I was more worried about myself. I am loud, crass, and very clumsy—not exactly a winning combination. I could only imagine what was going to go embarrassingly wrong.

As soon as we pulled up to the driveway, Ma came over and gave us both a hug. This was already very different from the formal handshakes that Erik endured when meeting my parents. Ma invited us in and showed us to the guest room. Within 10 minutes, Ma had us out by the pool and cocktails prepared. Over the years, I learned that this was a specialty of her's.

"This might not be so bad," I whispered to Erik, as Ma headed inside to grab some straws. "My mom and your mom are both alcoholics—they *do* have something in common to talk about!"

Erik elbowed me while unsuccessfully trying to supress a smile as Ma came back out.

"So, Sejal, you're Indian?"

"Yes. I was born there but I've lived here my whole life."

"Wow, that's so cool. The culture is just so beautiful."

This was the typical white person reaction that I was used to when asked about my background. However, nothing could have prepared me for what came next.

"Oh! Aren't your people the ones who go 'A-LA-LA-LA-LA-LA!' at weddings?" Ma made a piercing shrieking sound while also holding her right hand up in the air like she was holding a knife.

"Ma!" Erik said, laughing and turning red as he buried his face in his hands. "What the fuck?"

I immediately broke out in uncontrollable laughter at both Ma's question and at Erik blatantly cursing at her. "I don't think that's us," I finally managed to get out.

"Oh. Well I was staying at a hotel and there was an

Indian wedding there...I'm pretty sure that's what they do."

After what felt like a significantly long time, the doorbell rang and Erik's grandmother, Mema, trudged out to the patio. I knew that Mema was stubborn, frail, and had the voice of a teamster. Erik had also told me that Mema was a bit of a hussy and had quite the reputation at her nursing home. Mema's loving nickname in high school was Tits McGee and she had been arrested for skinny dipping at Horseneck Beach. I felt like I was about to meet a Blanche-Sophia hybrid with a Boston accent and I could not contain my excitement.

After the initial kisses and introductions, Ma suggested that we go in the pool.

"Oh, Sejal hates the sun," Erik said, outing me as the caramel vampire that I am. "She won't go in the pool."

"Why do ya hate the sun?" Mema asked, sounding like an extra on the cast of *The Departed.*

"Um, I don't know, I just hate to tan. I guess it might be cultural. In India, having lighter skin is a sign of beauty."

Without missing a beat, Mema drawled, "Oh....so ya must be considered really ugly where ya from."

"MEMA!" Erik was beyond mortified. Once again, I could not help but to dissolve into laughter.

As the afternoon progressed and drinks continued to flow freely, I really needed to pee. Mema was occupying the outside restroom and I figured I would wait. I had already embarrassed myself earlier that day by breaking a wine glass full of red wine all over their freshly painted patio. Normally my boobs in a bikini top could get me out of this situation, but I was told by several white friends that this was not the case with a boyfriend's family. I waited patiently until Mema proceeded to get out of the bathroom at a glacial pace.

I went into the bathroom and wiped front to back like a proper lady. As I held down to flush, it became clear why Mema was in the bathroom so long and it had *nothing* to do with her arthritis. The water began to come up from the bowl, along with my pee and used toilet paper. I ran out of the bathroom as the loud sloshing of the overflowing toilet surrounded the entire patio.

"Okay, I know what you're thinking," I panted, ankle deep in my own urine and watching my used toilet paper float by. "This time, it *really* wasn't my fault."

....

I met Erik's sister, Briannah, that evening as well. She came in, gave Erik a hug, said hi to me from a polite distance, and lit up a cigarette. I took an immediate liking to Briannah—she's my kind of people. Throughout the years, I would end up talking to Briannah more than Erik does and I find myself siding with her on 90% of things. At the time, Briannah was a single mom of two girls under the age of three. Briannah is under 30 and she now has three kids, a full time job, and the man of her dreams. Still, to this day, I have never met a mom who hustles, practices patience, and is as obsessed with her kids as she is.

Briannah has blessed us with three nieces. While they are adorable, the main blessing is that they fulfill the quota for grandchildren from Ma, who has left us alone on this subject since the birth of her third granddaughter. Most importantly, I have had time to mold the minds of my two eldest nieces, Ella and Lucy.

Ella and Lucy call me "Uncle Sejal," despite the fact that I have always made sure that my upper lip is as smooth as a baby's bottom every time I have seen them. Uncle Sejal has made peace with this nickname and has moved on to make sure that her minions know that nobody will ever be good enough for Uncle Erik when compared to her.

Recently, during our one year anniversary, Erik and I rented a cute cabin by the beach, about 20 minutes away from his family. The morning that we were planning to leave, I woke up and found a giant spider bite on my arm. I remembered feeling something on my arm during the night but I had disregarded it as one of my own hairs and fell back asleep. Erik was in the shower and I went into full panic mode as I found the guilty spider crawling on the floor and accidentally squished it. I put it in a Ziploc back and barged into the bathroom.

"Erik! I think it's poisonous! What should we do?"

Erik groaned and turned off the shower. He was used to my fits of hysteria and hypochondria but he still found them to be completely exhausting.

"I got bit by this spider! I need you to tell me if it's poisonous!" I thrusted the Ziploc bag at him. "It could be a brown recluse."

"It's not. It was a wolf spider or a funnel weaver," Erik sighed, putting on his towel and following me into the kitchen.

"It's probably poisonous because that's my luck—I was in Thailand for three months and I didn't get bit by a single spider but right after my first anniversary..." I proceeded to babble on as Erik examined the Ziploc with a frown on his face and reverse searched the image on his phone.

"Well, it's not poisonous. It's a funnel weaver. Look, Google says so as well."

I looked from Erik's phone to the spider in the bag as my heart rate slowly returned to normal. I nodded curtly and then snatched the bag and shoved it in my Michael Kors bag.

"I'm going to take it with me to brunch so—"

"I don't even want to know," Erik cut me off.

When we arrived at Ma's house, I filled in everybody (even though nobody asked) on the spider situation. I then slammed the Ziploc with the aforementioned specimen onto the dining table.

"Ew! You brought it with you?!" Ma said, making the same face she did when she looked at Indian food.

"Of COURSE I did! What if it's poisonous and Erik misidentified the species? Hmm? Then this spider, right here, is the key to getting an antidote in a timely manner."

As usual, everyone just turned their backs and ignored me. I turned my attention to Ella and Lucy, who were examining the Ziploc with fascination.

"Listen, girls. I need you to understand something: your Uncle Erik is a hussy."

Ella and Lucy blinked at me, not comprehending what I was saying.

"Don't worry, I'll teach you that word when you're older. My point is, Uncle Erik will be quick to replace me."

"Where are ya goin'?" Lucy asked.

"EXACTLY, Luce. It's up to you two to make sure I don't go anywhere, no matter what happens. Look, if your beloved Uncle Sejal happens to die a tragic death from this spider bite, then it's up to you two to ensure that whatever bimbo Erik brings around knows her place. Capeesh?"

Ella and Lucy eagerly nodded as I went on.

"So, when Uncle Erik brings home another woman that is not me, you need to be prepared. Tell her things like 'You're not as pretty as Uncle Erik's wife' or 'Did you know Sejal was getting her PhD? Are you that smart?' You know, tell her things that let her know that she will never be as good as me. Also, I would like you to constantly remind her that Uncle Erik will always love me more."

Ella and Lucy seemed to be game for this when Briannah came up and asked me what I was doing.

"I'm telling them what to do in case I die."

Briannah smirked and rolled her eyes. I waited until she was a safe distance before leaning in and whispering, "And, whatever you do girls, don't accept any candy from Uncle Erik's next woman. It's poison...she'll be trying to get you two out of the picture."

....

Melvin has always wanted to be a part of a proposal. If he had it his way, he would have been there when my brother proposed to his girlfriend and when Erik proposed to me. Melvin is a huge ball of mush and is the most optimistic person in the world—I told Erik plenty of times that if he ever proposed, to make sure Melvin was hours away because his positivity would be a mood kill.

I don't like to give credit to Erik for being romantic because I enjoy my reign as Queen of Romance. To be clear, I am the least romantic person. I frequently (more than Erik would ever admit) just turn to him, put my hand on his penis, and say, "Wanna smash?" This is my idea of romance. However, I am very competitive—I want to constantly show Erik (and everyone) that whatever he can do as a romantic gesture, I can top it a thousandfold. I will concede that Erik wins at proposals—but only because I haven't had a chance to propose myself.

Erik proposed to me in June 2016 at Devil's Den, a pre-historic underground spring in Florida. While I was expecting a proposal in the future, I had no clue that he was going to propose during this trip. A few months before, Erik had asked my parents and Dadaji for permission to propose. I think this is one of the few customs that brown people and white people can agree on: you don't just propose to someone, you ask their family for permission. Erik had nearly thrown up at lunch (which I was not invited to) when he asked. After he asked, my mom broke out in happy sobs that someone was willing to marry me despite my tattoos. Dadaji and Melvin were just as relieved that a man was interested in spending his life with me.

The week leading up to the proposal, I was just excited about our trip. I had wanted to go to Devil's Den for years and we had finally successfully planned a trip. I did not expect a proposal, primarily because I was not in my prime. Whenever I finish finals, several bizarre things happen to my body all at the same time. Sure enough, like a Swiss watch, my appearance was in the following dilapidated state: 1) My hair had started to vaguely resemble a bird's nest—I was fairly certain there were at least a few magpies building their home in there; 2) My left eye developed a bizarre nervous twitch that made me think Botox was the next logical step; and 3) there was a cystic pimple growing on my forehead—this thing was deep, it had roots, and I had named it Grover.

I know that you are thinking that a pimple cannot possibly be that bad. Let me put it this way: Dazzo, Erik's best friend, ran into us at the grocery store. Upon seeing the monstrosity on my forehead, he jumped back and said, "Holy shit! What happened to you? Were you in an accident?" Dazzo is a dick but this was a moment when he was actually showing genuine concern—*that's* how bad Grover was.

While I did possibly suspect Erik might propose, due to unsubtle cues from Daniela asking me to go get a manicure (something I never do) with her, the morning of the trip to the springs, all of those suspicions were put aside. Erik was in an extraordinarily bad mood and his face had the same expression as a pug who had just sucked on a lemon. While I would later learn that this was due to nerves, at the time I assumed it was because I insisted that we leave extra early. Ma had been begging Erik for a nice photo of us to frame and I figured if we got to Devil's Den early enough, the staff members might be willing to take pictures of us in the empty springs.

When we got to Devil's Den, Erik was easily able to persuade the staff members to let us into the springs early. We got into the springs and I realized my long skirt was a mistake, as the rain had flooded the water above the wooden platform. As the staff member took posed pictures from the top of the stairs and I was shivering from the cold water/the throbbing headache thanks to Grover, I knew Erik would never propose there—I am the clumsiest person most people know and there was 200 feet of crystal blue water below me.

Sure enough, as the staff member continued to take pictures, Erik got down on one knee. When Erik finished his speech, he asked, "Will you marry me?"

"Wait," I said, completely serious. "Are you proposing to me or to this planet growing on my forehead?"

8. POPCORN IN A RAISIN BOWL

There's a lot of things that Indians don't tell you about their weddings. One of the most important things to remember is this: for Americans, the wedding is all about the bride and the groom; for Indians, the wedding is about everyone *except* the bride and the groom. Indian weddings are not meant to represent the love between two people—rather, they signify the love of two families coming together. This holds true for all Indian people unless you are me—if you are me, then your wedding is all about Melvin.

Melvin was a complete bridezilla during the entire wedding. Yes, he was doting and gave in to some of my bizarre requests (like having a sushi station at my bridal shower and having a *Harry Potter* themed Sangeet). However, Melvin was quick to lay down the law on whatever he wanted and, if I protested, he would repeatedly bark, "It's. My. Special. DAY!"

I was determined to do all of my wedding shopping online, including buying my own saris and those for my 14 bridesmaids. Melvin insisted that we needed to buy all clothing, jewelry, and invitations from India. I put up a fight but was unsuccessful. In December 2016, my mom and I headed to the motherland.

When Pri, who I had chosen as my Maid of Honor, found out that my mom and I were headed to India, she instantly booked a ticket. Pri hates going to India more than me and I was extremely shocked that she was willing to travel over 7,500 miles to do something we both detested: shopping.

"I have to go with them! They need me!" Pri had told her mom. This was the moment I knew that there was no better choice for Maid of Honor.

Pri met us at Dubai International Airport from her connecting Chicago flight. As we were getting ready to board, there was a seat available in business class. I told Pri to take it. I am a complete waste of a good seat on an airplane. I will only ever fly coach because I sleep from takeoff to landing, only waking up to use the bathroom or to eat. Anyone who has traveled with me knows that I will sleep for 16 hours at a time on a plane, wake up to disembark, get on my next flight, and keep sleeping.

When we landed in India, we were given less than 24 hours to rest before braving our way to the bazaars to begin wedding shopping. Despite that I never had a Pinterest prior to this, I have always been a planner and I already had a folder with the wedding palette, invitation designs, and sari styles I preferred.

I knew that all of this was a waste as this was not my first rodeo. The Indian bridal store experience is the opposite of the American one: the employees at the bridal boutiques are pushy, loud, and messy. There are no fancy chairs or champagne—you sit on mattresses on the floor and are offered bottled water. Even more, when you show them the outfits and colors you desire, they will always bring you the opposite of that, even if it costs less. There's no rhyme or reason for this blatant disregard, it's just one of those odd national quirks that everyone is okay with—everyone except for me.

"I want neutral, blush colored saris for the bridesmaids," I explained in Gujarati, showing several swatches and sample pictures to the employee. "No bright colors or colors that look like Pepto-Bismol. And I don't want a lot of work," I added, letting him know that tons of sequins and beads would not be appreciated.

"I've got just the thing, Madame," the employee said, giving me a quick Indian head bobble before disappearing into a back room. He returned with a stack of saris going well above his head. When he laid them out, all of the saris were hot pink and were shinier than the Las Vegas Strip at night.

This same interaction was repeated over the course of 12 hours each day for the next six days. Every morning, Pri would pop an Adderall and I would pop a Xanax just so we could make it through the day. Pri was the ultimate champ during all of this—she provided comedic relief, continuously showed me cute videos on Instagram, and helped me in and out of so many saris that I lost count. Also, given that Pri and I both hate shopping, within six days we were able to find all five of my outfits (plus an extra 10 as backups), Pri's saris, 14 bridesmaids' saris, and 12 outfits for Erik. I have always been a fast, savvy shopper, but nothing compared to this experience —my mom, Pri, and myself made for a quick, decisive, and strategic team.

Pri left India after seven days, while I was stuck there for another six days without her. During this time, I became immensely depressed as I hated being in India alone. The only company I had in my room was a pigeon that had gone into the air conditioning vent. By the sound of it, by day 10 in India, the pigeon had begun to roost and its incessant cooing made me have homicidal thoughts at 3:00 AM as I would lie in bed, craving a pigeon pie. There were blonde tumbleweeds of Pri's hair that would randomly blow by on the marble floor and I would never pick them up—I sat there for a good 15 minutes at one point, watching the blonde tumbleweed float by as my eyes filled with tears and I thought of Pri.

My mom told me that after we went to the invitation printers in Vadodara, we needed to get jewelry from one of the stores there. The two hour car ride there at the break of dawn was already challenging enough. I scratched at my head and my forehead, feeling myself breaking out in hives as I prepared for even more shopping.

"What's wrong?" my mom asked. "*Jū*?"

"Huh?" I asked not comprehending.

"Lice! It means lice. Do you have it?"

"That sounds extremely anti-Semitic, Mom."

My mom rolled her eyes and went back to playing Sudoku on her phone.

When we got to the printers, I quickly realized that they were no better than the clothing merchants in Ahmedabad. The lady kept showing me pictures of really religious invitations, with pictures of Ganesh and Shreenathji.

"Mom, we can't do this!" I yelled, pointing at the pile of samples.

"Why not? It looks very nice," she said, picking up one of the invitations and beaming with approval.

"Because this isn't just an Indian wedding. This is a hybrid wedding and all of these white people are going to look at Ganesh and Shreenathji and wonder, 'What's with the elephant and the black guy on these invitations?'"

"Okay, *beta*, then let's do one with Shri Krishna. See? It's classy."

I used my phone and pulled up Google Images. "Yeah, that's great, Mom. Then people will just think I put an overgrown Smurf dressed in drag on the invites."

"Oh," Mom said, looking at a picture of a Smurf. "But that's cartoon—this is real!"

About an hour later, the invitations were set. I had settled on a small, abstract picture of Ganesh and we were headed to the jewelry store. When we pulled up to the store, I realized that this would also be a different experience than going to Jared's. The "store" was a mansion and had a heavy Grecian vibe to it, with large marble statues of lions and women with their arms cut off. The building was surrounded by several security guards, all handling AK-47s.

What in the curry fuck was I in for, you may wonder? The answer is this: mind numbing boredom. I do not enjoy shopping for clothes much less shopping for jewelry. Each set was gaudy and something that I would never wear again for the rest of my life. Seeing as Erik and I were not having kids, I could not figure out what the appeal of this jewelry would even be. As my mom and the jeweler looked over another set that looked like it could weigh down a baby elephant, I asked to be excused so that I could use the restroom.

The restroom at this boutique jeweler was, in one word, atrocious—this restroom was the reason that the UN created a World Toilet Day. The restroom had no air conditioning, unlike the rest of the building, and had one flickering dim light bulb. The toilet seat was covered in urine and the entire bathroom smelled like bird poop, even though there were no birds, or windows for that matter, in sight. I hovered over the toilet and peed as quickly as I could, trying to not pass out from holding my breath. As my stream slowed down to a trickle, I realized I had made the ultimate rookie mistake in India—I had not assessed my toilet paper rations before going into the restroom. Under normal circumstances, I would have dripped dry, but seeing as I was going to be putting on a very skimpy thong after, I decided that this wasn't an option.

I looked around in vain, knowing this restroom would never have toilet paper (not that I would be remotely comfortable using it even if they did have it). My eyes spotted the makeshift bidet, which was a bucket of film-covered water and a container with a handle bobbing inside of it. I frantically searched my purse and the only thing I could find was a single Orbit gum wrapper. I sighed and used the tiny wrapper to blot before dropping the wrapper in the toilet and dousing myself in hand sanitizer in the hallway. I quickly pulled out my phone and sent Erik what I thought was a racy text:

Me: My vagina smells like spearmint. Miss me yet?

....

American brides get a special day—Indian brides get a special week (or, in my case, 12 days). Indian people always want to do everything bigger and better than their Western counterparts and weddings are their time to truly shine. If you're Indian and you've ever told a white person that you are Indian, some variation of this is undoubtedly said to you within three minutes: "Don't you guys have weddings that are, like, a week long? Oh my god, I've always wanted to go to an Indian wedding. Indian weddings are so beautiful with all the colors!"

The truth is, there is so much that goes into planning an Indian wedding that, unless you're Priyanka Chopra, you don't realize the extent of it until you are planning your own wedding. In the months leading up to my wedding, uncles and aunties from all over would come over on the weekends to fill out the wedding invitations and help with the mailing out. Bijal, my aunt in New Jersey, volunteered to make me a custom bouquet made out of the pages of a *Harry Potter* book. Neel had taken on the role of being the day-of coordinator. My cousin and my aunts came the day before the bridal shower and helped me to decorate the entire back patio to fit my "Rosé & Slay [Before the Big Day]" theme. My mom had taken over planning and making treats for all guest gift bags for each hotel room.

And then there was Melvin the Bridezilla. Erik was a restaurant manager at the time and I was used to him being gone 14+ hours a day and always working weekends. This meant that other than one viewing of the venue, helping me mail out his side of the family's invitations, and one visit to the caterer, Erik was not involved in any planning. Melvin was there for me from beginning to end. It was Melvin who helped me to create the menus for various nights, pick out decorations, finalize the venue, and coordinate the entire event. To this day, three years later, my friends still ask if they can hire Melvin as their wedding planner. I always caution my friends that while Melvin did an exceptional job planning my wedding, he has one major shortcoming: the seating chart.

Melvin was adamant on having the reception separated by side, with one side being my family and other side being Erik's family.

"Dad, that's not going to work," I pointed out. "There are like 250 family members, not even including my friends. Erik's side is only going to have 20 people!"

"That's not a problem," Melvin quickly told me, pulling out a handwritten blueprint he had made at some point. "We can just throw all of your friends on that side along with any mutual friends. That should even it out."

"Okay," I said, frowning as I looked at this blueprint, "but now the wedding looks like it took place in the 1960s. What, do we have our own separate water fountains, too?!"

Sana and several other aunts and uncles eventually helped me to persuade Melvin that separate sides would not work for a wedding where the ratio of white people to Indian people was so drastically different. I figured it was better to pepper white people all over the wedding, therefore making them feel more comfortable and making the pictures look less like something that Rosa Parks would disapprove of. I showed my mother-in-law the final seating plan for the wedding when she was visiting for the bridal shower.

"Oh my god!" Ma exclaimed, trying to make sense of all the Indian names. "We're going to look like pieces of popcorn in a raisin bowl!"

....

For the 10 nights leading up to my wedding day, I had been averaging less than four hours of sleep. Every night, we had friends and family come to the house from 6:00 PM onward to drink and eat for hours on end. Afterwards, myself, Erik, and the gang of cousins would head to the Airbnb 10 minutes away that my parents had rented—despite that we were the bride and groom, since my parents' house was packed to the brim with family members, we were the first to be booted along with all of the other "youngsters." We spent the majority of these nights bar hopping and then returning to the Airbnb to drink and get high.

The night before the wedding, I had gotten a whole two hours of sleep. The previous night had been the Sangeet, which is like a rehearsal dinner, but much, much better. The Sangeet is basically like a rehearsal reception—there's drinking, dancing, and all around debauchery. After the Sangeet ended and all 280 people invited (of the 350 guests) began to disperse, I ended up at the inside bar, where I met all of my uncles on my mom's side. While my mom has always been close to her side of the family, they mostly live up north and I saw them maybe once every five years on random visits. As my uncles introduced themselves, I tried to keep track of who was related and how—one guy was my mom's mom's brother's cousin's son and another was my mom's uncle's nephew (I'm pretty sure this was the same person, but I was too drunk to be certain).

I made my way to bed at 3:00 AM and snuggled up to Pri. Seeing as Erik and I were not "officially" married, he had to share a double twin room with Dazzo, his best man, while Pri and I got the presidential suite for the night. I felt bizarrely secure, knowing that nothing could go wrong as long as Melvin the Bridezilla and I were in charge. I had even made an 11-page itinerary, complete with scheduled timelines and maps for all of our white friends and family. Nothing could go wrong. I quietly drifted off to sleep, completely unaware of what the next morning had in store for me.

I had to force myself to wake up at 5:00 AM. The wedding did not start until 9:00 AM but I had to take into account the hair, makeup, getting dressed, and the photographs. The bridesmaids all slowly trudged in to get ready, each one looking more exhausted than the next. Sleeza and Luna delivered champagne and vodka, as expected. Justine came in looking like the Filipina Princess that she is, even before putting makeup on.

"Don't stand so close to me," I told Justine, rubbing the two bruised ball sacks under my eyes. "It's bad for my self-esteem."

Lauren was the last of the bridesmaids to arrive. When I opened the door, I saw something was severely wrong. Her eyes were as puffy as mine but were bloodshot beyond oblivion and her voice sounded like a 70-year-old smoker.

"What's wrong?"

"I can't get Elsie up," Lauren somehow managed to croak. "I'm sorry."

Lauren informed me that Elsie had gone on a bender the night before and had somehow done so much cocaine that no amount of blackout drunk could make her fall asleep. She had spent the entire night screaming and crying. Lizzy left the room and asked Marco and Nick to crash in their room, leaving Lauren alone to deal with Elsie's breakdown. Apparently, Elsie's boyfriend had broken up with her that night.

"It's ironic," I said, inviting her in and patting her on the back. "I told Elsie and Bert the best present they could get me for my wedding was for them to break-up. Be careful what you wish for, huh?"

"S-s-so you don't want me to go back and try to wake her up?" Lauren half sniffled as she drew in another rattly breath.

I waved Lauren off. "Nah. She'll still be as high as a kite even if we can wake her up. Best place for her is in the hotel room so she doesn't make a scene. I'll just reconfigure the entrance walking pairs for the party."

As the makeup artist literally painted on my face and made me look presentable, I sipped on my champagne and calmly started rearranging the bridesmaids and groomsmen pairings for the entrances. I realized that we were behind schedule and texted the photographer, letting him know that I did not want any pictures of the bridal party getting ready.

"Are you okay?" Pri asked me.

Pri looked genuinely concerned about my calm demeanor. The truth is, I was an eerily zen bride. Whatever went wrong that day, no matter how big or how small, I could not have cared less. Even throughout the planning process, when I couldn't get the date or venue or decorator that I wanted, I just learned to roll with it. There's this misconception, especially with American brides, that your wedding is the best day of your life—for Indian brides, your wedding is a celebration that signifies the kick-off to the best days yet to come. The trick to being a cool, collected bride is to remember this...and also to be severely sleep deprived and dehydrated, therefore being too tired to honestly give a damn. A steady dose of alcohol and Xanax also helps.

That being said, there was no amount of alcohol or Xanax large enough to help me deal with our photographer. My parents had booked Amir because he had done my other cousins' weddings that same year. To this day, I am convinced we only booked with him because we got a Groupon deal that was 3-weddings-for-the-price-of-1. Amir was extremely talented and created stunning photos—however, he was also pushy, demanding, and far too involved.

Amir was definitely disappointed in me as a bride, and not just because I did not share his enthusiasm for first look or the bridal party getting ready photos. I made it clear to Amir that I had very strict guidelines, like the fact that I did not want pictures of anyone eating food. For some reason, at all Indian weddings, photographers take pictures of everyone shoveling food in their mouths. Indian people eat with their hands and while your 90-year-old great grandmother is cute, it is so gross to see her eating with her dentures on a bread plate nearby.

Another one of my requests to Amir was to not take any pictures of Erik's mom's boyfriend. Ma had gotten a divorce out of the blue four months before the wedding. When I sent her the invitation, she asked for a plus one for her new boyfriend because she would, and I quote, "feel lonely" if she didn't have a date. I wanted to point out there would be 349 other people at the wedding for company, including her extended family. Instead, I chose the high road: I found her boyfriend on Facebook, showed Amir the pictures, and told him that Ma's boyfriend was not to be in any photographs or video footage.

After getting ready and coming downstairs, Amir was immediately in action mode. He wanted so many pictures of the bridesmaids and groomsmen outside, in the humid/scorching Florida summer, that we were all drenched in sweat. He kept telling Erik and I to lean in and pretend to kiss "but, whatever you do, do not actually kiss." After over 40 minutes, he had let the rest of the party go but insisted that I pose for solo bridal shots. I let him go on for a full five minutes and then told him to stop.

"But, if we don't take a bunch, you won't get the perfect shot like the other brides."

"I don't care," I said flatly. "I'm tired and hungry. I need to eat before this wedding."

"But, Indian brides aren't supposed to eat anything before the wedding ceremony!"

I left Amir in the dust and headed to meet my bridal party. Justine and Ana had gotten me a bacon, egg, and cheese croissant. I could have cried from joy if I hadn't been so dehydrated. As I crammed the business end of the croissant into my mouth, my cheeks looking like a chipmunk's, a random aunty who I had never seen before looked at me and gave a purposeful stare.

"Indian brides never eat the morning of their wedding," the aunty said, slightly smiling, before walking away.

"I'M HUNGRY!" I shouted, my yell muffled as bits of bacon spit out of my mouth.

Months later, I asked my parents why people kept telling me not to eat. Melvin told me that since Indian weddings last for hours and used to be outdoors in the old days, nobody would eat the morning of the event so as to avoid having to poop mid-ceremony. To this day, I am convinced Melvin is making this up but it's not like I have a better explanation for it.

When I made the walk up the aisle, I could not stop smiling the biggest smile ever. *This is it,* I kept saying to myself. *I'm finally getting rid of these doofuses!* My uncles, who were walking me down the aisle, kept telling me not to smile, that an Indian bride never smiles. I started to wonder what an Indian bride *was* allowed to do. I got to the altar and took my seat, trying to make out Erik's face through the *antarpat*, a shawl that separates the bride and groom from seeing each other. When the *antarpat* was finally lifted, I saw to my horror that Erik, my mom, and Melvin all were crying.

"Oh my god, are you guys *crying*?!" I hissed. "Tighten up, bozos!"

Melvin's face quickly turned sour—only I could put a damper on Melvin's special day so quickly. Our family priest performed the ceremony. I could barely understand anything the priest said. Erik would turn to me and ask what was going on, I would shrug cluelessly, and the priest would repeat himself, each time getting more and more angry. Luna and Sleeza continuously came up to give me sips of vodka from a Starbucks coffee container, resulting in me accidentally kicking the coconut that had a swastika painted on it. The swastika is a symbol for prosperity in the Hindu culture and it dates back way before the Nazis decided to use it. The coconut was from Whole Foods and I'm not sure what it represents, my aunties just kept saying, "It's symbolic."

I always knew Indian weddings had strange customs, but there were many that I was not aware of. I knew about the one where the bride's side tries to steal the groom's shoes to make him give them money (I once had my sari ripped trying to protect a pair of my cousin's shoes at his wedding). Nobody prepared me for the amount of sweets that strange family members shove in your mouth or the fact that all of my aunts whisper some nonsense in Erik's ear and give him money. The strangest of this tradition was the one where my brother and cousins had to grab Erik's toe and refuse to let go until cash was given. Seeing as Erik and I did not bring wallets to the altar, my mom handed Dazzo a fistful of cash. Instead of handing the money to my brother, Dazzo decided to make it rain like we were in a Tijuana strip club.

While we all laughed, I caught the death stare of the priest. He was not amused and sharply told my brother to just take the money and leave. I am convinced that this priest will never do another interracial wedding after ours.

Immediately after the wedding, Erik and I ordered a pizza from room service, scarfed it down, and passed out. We didn't get up until Melvin repeatedly called us, asking if we were almost ready. It was at that point I realized that I had missed calls from my hair and makeup team. Erik scrambled to his room to go get dressed and I ran over to wake up Pri. I was running on fumes already and could feel my stomach grumbling for sustenance. Somehow, I powered through and made it in time for the majority of the cocktail hour, which was a pregame for the actual reception. Somehow, even Elsie, although looking slightly roughed up, was more punctual to the cocktail hour.

As I posed for pictures and downed about three vodka tonics, I realized that I had to pee right before the reception started. Seeing as my sari was essentially a ballgown, I recruited Pari to help me this time (another aunt had already had to help me go to the bathroom in my wedding sari that morning). Pari dutifully walked me to the restroom, which was crowded with various aunties and cousins who I had never met. The handicap stall, the only one big enough to hold the two of us, was preoccupied by someone's grandmother.

"I can't wait," I told Pari, giving her a meaningful

look.

Pari nodded and helped to lift up my sari and pull down my thong. I sat on the toilet, door wide open to all these strangers, and started to pee in one of the regular stalls.

"You know," I said, unspooling some toilet paper, "I stopped eating asparagus a week ago as a courtesy. You're welcome."

....

Erik and I got approximately 45 minutes of sleep before having to head to the airport for our honeymoon flight. After the reception, about 60 of our friends and cousins went to the hotel bar until we were asked to leave by the disgruntled bartenders. At this point, everyone went to the presidential suite and we drank and smoked more than was possibly healthy—we were at the peak of the 10 day bender.

Upon returning to the suite, we learned that Melvin had the bed decorated with rose petals that spelled out our initials inside of a heart—this was a huge buzzkill and probably the main reason that Erik and I did not have sex on our wedding night. The other reason was that there were 60 people in the suite and even after they all left, Nick insisted that he be allowed to sleep in one of the bedrooms in the suite.

"Come on, Sej," he pleaded. "It's not like you're going to use all the rooms! Please?"

"Whatever, I really don't care."

Erik and I arrived at the airport starving and dehydrated. Neither one of us got to eat more than two bites of the dinner from the reception. The buffet attendants had started to clear out the items and Melvin all but yelled at them that he had paid for the food and that the bride and groom needed to eat. Once we loaded up our plates and returned to the sweetheart table, we had gotten distracted by people coming up to give us hugs and money—I don't like hugs, but I love money, so, naturally I was eager to get up. Somehow our plates got taken away by a staff member who I hope lost their job.

Needless to say, Erik and I did not look anything like the glowing, happy newlyweds you see on TV. We both passed out waiting to board the flight and then promptly fell asleep on the plane. When the flight attendant came by to offer a beverage, we both eagerly licked our chapped, flaking lips like refugees and chugged the water.

"Oh, are you two newlyweds?" she asked, eyeing the henna on my arms. "You should have said something, we could have upgraded you for free! Maybe I can bring by some champ—"

"No!" Erik and I both barked as we nestled back to sleep.

When we landed in the Dominican Republic, Erik and I looked like two feral cats that had been on the losing end of an alley fight. The flight attendant gave us a weak smile as we hobbled off the plane. It took nearly two hours to finally get settled into our resort. A lot of people ask me about our first night on the honeymoon and I find this extremely creepy—we are all adults, we have sex, okay? There are no surprises that I need to share with anyone. However, everyone who asks is more disturbed when I tell them the truth about our honeymoon night: Erik and I ordered room service, ate pizza in bed, and fell asleep by 8:30 PM watching *Rush Hour 2*.

I disconnected from the wifi at the resort for the

majority of our stay. I was exhausted from socializing with 350 guests and needed a break from all of the texts and social media notifications. Erik and I finally got a chance to hydrate, eat, and plot our revenge.

The majority of our honeymoon consisted of thinking of ways to get back at Marco for his god awful speech. Marco was already on Melvin's shit list because he ditched the wedding early to go to take a nap. Consequently, he woke up about 15 minutes before the reception, where he was to make a speech. I had an emergency speech written out for him weeks in advance, but, true to form, he declined and decided to go with his own sordid ramblings.

Marco's speech started out normal—talking about all the ways he annoyed me as an older brother and how we became close over the years. He then proceeded to tell everyone that he ate a bunch of mushrooms on a pizza his first night meeting Erik and how his friends had offered Erik $82 to do pushups with a roman candle, lit aflame, between his butt cheeks (an offer Erik accepted and that there is still video proof of online). This story was slightly mortifying because all of Erik's bosses at the time were present at the wedding and this did not help his professional image. However, on the bright side, the majority of the Indian aunties and uncles did not understand that my brother was referencing taking drugs—rather, they just assumed he had eaten a mushroom pizza and a sea of approving Indian head bobbles confirmed this.

The speech then took a very bizarre turn and is the reason that people to this day only talk about Marco's speech when reflecting back on our giant blowout of an Indian wedding. Marco proceeded to start talking about alcohol and its various dangers. "You know, people use alcohol as a social curtain...so don't do that." I was certain that my brother was on drugs and turned to my cousins, asking if they had smoked him out. They all shook their heads and, judging by the shocked look on their faces, they were telling the truth. Marco then told us to read books and not watch too much TV, and to focus on self-developmental TED Talks. This is rich coming from Marco, especially seeing as three years earlier he had sent me this little gem:

Marco: Do you get a discount on books?
Me: What kind of books?
Marco: Chapter books.
Me: What the fuck. Chapter books? You mean like regular books from the bookstore?
Marco: Yeah, like normal books.
Me: I get a discount with my Barnes & Noble membership.
Marco: Word. I need some books.
Me: Okay. You should probably just get one at a time. You have a tendency not to finish them.

After Marco prattled on for a solid 15 minutes, I finally asked him to wrap it up and signaled to the DJ to play some wrap-up music like they do at the Oscars. Since this scene, Erik and I were hellbent on Marco getting his comeuppance. Even when I didn't get some of the vendors I wanted, Ma insisted on her having a date that we never met at her son's wedding, and Elsie went MIA right before the wedding—none of this has haunted me the way that Marco's speech has.

Erik and I decided that at Marco's future wedding, we would be making a toast together. To this day, we have compiled dozens of videos and have even interviewed his friends for extra stories. I look forward to the day that our toast will overshadow the abortion of a speech that Marco gave at our wedding. I stand by the fact that while I was not a bridezilla, I was and still am an extremely vengeful bride—think of me as Uma Thurman a la *Kill Bill*, except instead of ninja-like reflexes and swords, I use gut-wrenching insults to destroy those who have wronged me.

9. WONDER BREAD GOES ABROAD

There are some things that couples should discuss before marriage or even before getting into a committed relationship—values, money, goals, etc. However, based on my experience with Erik, the one thing that I urge all of you to ask your significant other is this: do they like machines? If they answer yes, then take a few weeks apart and really think about what you're getting yourself into.

At a family dinner, Melvin decided to bring up a new type of plane model that was going to be used by Delta. Erik immediately jumped in the conversation and proceeded to prattle on about every detail of this plane —the engine, wingspan, flight capabilities, and god only knows what else. After 10 minutes straight, Erik turned to see Marco and me staring at him with looks of abject disgust and mild intrigue on our faces.

"What? I like machines!" Erik said, shrugging.

Like machines was a huge understatement. Erik is obsessed with all types of machines, specifically anything travel related. After that initial conversation, I still had no idea just how intense his love for machines ran. Then, I surprised him with a cruise for his 30th birthday. Erik was jazzed to be doing something "overseas" and I was excited as this was our big first trip outside together.

My enthusiasm was quashed within 10 minutes on the ship. I wanted to relax in the room where I had two bottles of champagne delivered on ice for our arrival. Erik, on the other hand, insisted that we report to our muster station for the mandatory drill.

"Nobody will know if we aren't there!" I whined. "If they say anything, I'll just tell them that I have severe food poisoning and couldn't get off the toilet. Diarrhea, Erik—*nobody* ever questions diarrhea!"

Erik was adamant and made me stand outside in the sun for the full 45 minutes of the muster drill, during which I comprehended little to no information about safety procedures. I stared into the water and licked my lips with thirst, thinking of an ice cold cocktail. My entire plan during the cruise had been to only drink rum out of various hollowed out fruits. Erik's plan had been to learn every feature of this cruise ship. Right after the muster drill, as I was making a beeline for the bar, Erik picked up a pamphlet full of engineering facts about the ship. I don't know what bozo is responsible for creating those pamphlets, but I need to tell them this: stop it. You are single-handedly ruining cruises for the rest of us normal people.

Erik and I had gotten on the cruise with a goal to have a threesome. We figured it was the best way to kick off this new decade in his life and, since I am what I like to refer to as a "third of a gay," this was the perfect chance to meet a svelte vixen that we would never have to see again after the cruise.

During our first morning on the ship, Erik and I laid out in the adults only pool area to scope out our prospects. I am not exaggerating when I say that we were on the ugliest cruise ever. Every single woman looked like an obese house frau that had escaped from a 1600s German portrait of farm life. They were dumpy, frowning, and constantly greased up from tanning oil that was not doing their splotchy skin any favors.

There was one couple who took far too much of an interest in us. Well, I wouldn't call them a couple so much as two people whose week-long fling we got to see blossom from the beginning. We met Ben at a wine bar during our first night there. He sat down and smiled at us before deciding to strike up a conversation. I figured he must have been stuck on a miserable family vacation and, while neither one of us were into double-penetration, the least Erik and I could do was talk to him.

About five minutes into our conversation, a little kid who was maybe 10 came up to Ben and asked, "Dad, can I get some candy?"

"Sure," Ben said, handing the kid a $20 bill.

I found this to be admirable—being stuck on a cruise with your family is tough. Ben had the right idea: throw your kid some money and let the rest of the family members take care of the little miscreant. It was at this point that Jenna, a boozehound of a blonde, began to mosey over to Ben.

"Hiiiiiiii," Jenna drawled.

Ben seemed quite smitten with Jenna from the get-go. Ben quickly ditched us and sidled up to Jenna to talk about some inane subject. I saw Ben's kid standing outside of the wine bar, shoveling Twizzlers into his mouth and watching his dad mack on this drunk stranger. I shot Erik an appalled look—this man was on a cruise, alone, with his son, and had chosen to cozy up to a knock-off Madonna with a chunkier body. Not to mention, his son chose $20 of *Twizzlers* from the candy shop onboard—there were at least 2,000 better options than that.

Over the next seven nights, Erik and I continued to randomly bump into Ben and Jenna, both of whom got progressively more drunk and PDA-prone. I never saw Ben's son again and whenever I would ask about him, Ben would casually waive me off, telling me that his son was at a kid's club onboard where there was free babysitting. Erik and I tried to dodge Ben and Jenna each night —we were already surrounded by so many gross looking people, we didn't need two more. However, without fail, Ben and Jenna would find us on the shrinking cruise ship every night and force us to watch them drunkenly mash their teeth together in a half-assed attempt at making out.

Since a threesome was clearly not happening based on the caliber of guests on the ship, the entire cruise was muddled by Erik's need to become one with machines. I am 100% confident that if there was a robot uprising, Erik would be the traitor who would commit treason and side with the cyborgs. Since I could never read the map or remember where anything was on the cruise ship, Erik would walk around with a large, folded out map at all times (trust me, nobody was more embarrassed than me). As I walked, Erik would bark, "Go aft!"

"What? What are you saying?"

"We are going aft! Not starboard! AFT!" Erik would keep yelling at me over the wind.

"I don't understand the words coming out of your mouth. Use English." I felt like Chris Rock trying to understand Jackie Chan.

"Just go down, Sejal. Straight down." Erik would

sigh, shaking his head and hanging it low in disappointment, as if *I* was the one embarrassing *him* in this situation.

On his actual birthday, Erik had a special request. When he first told me this, my ears perked up. *Finally,* I thought. *Sexual favors are my forté. Now this I can get onboard with.* Ugh, *onboard*? Even I had started making nautical puns thanks to Erik constantly telling me boat facts at all hours of the day. I hated myself and Erik so much in that moment.

"I want to watch planes land."

"What?!" I burst out into a fit of giggles, convinced that Erik was trying to make me upset. "Okay, yeah, sure, and while we are at it, we can count the grains of sand on the beach."

"I'm serious. At Maho Beach we can sit down and watch the planes land. It's really cool!"

Erik pulled out yet another pamphlet and I was convinced he had his own printing press hidden in the room somewhere. Erik leafed through the pamphlet and showed me various planes landing near a beach.

"B-b-but...it's St. Maarten," I whispered, choking back tears.

I will admit that watching the planes land at Maho Beach was actually pretty cool. This is primarily because the planes get extremely low to the ground and you can see several people fall over on the beach each time. I thoroughly enjoyed myself once I realized there was a bar right on the beach and I had a seat in the shade to watch. Sipping on a coconut full of rum and watching bikini-clad girls and shirtless jocks faceplant in the sand was therapeutic for me. As a bonus, the loud sound of the planes flying down low made it impossible for me to hear Erik telling me facts about each type of plane. On the downside, Erik took approximately 168 pictures of planes landing and only two of me sitting by the beach.

When we got back on the boat, it was nearly sunset. While I am generally horny for 22 out of 24 hours a day, on this day I was feeling exceptionally amorous as the sun and the drinks had gone to my head. As Erik and I peered out at the island and the ship began to disembark, I leaned over suggestively and coyly said, "How about we head back to the room for a bit? I can think of a present you haven't unwrapped yet." (I know, not my best line—but, hey, it was 97°F outside and I had consumed about eight coconuts full of rum).

"I want to look at the propellers," Erik said without a hint of humor in his voice. He quickly started moving towards the stern of the boat.

"Excuse me?"

"The propellers, Sejal! I want to see the propellers go as we leave the port!"

Ladies, if you're ever feeling bad about yourself, just remember this: my sausage pocket had been turned down for a rusty set of propellers on a Royal Caribbean cruise line.

....

As our honeymoon to the Dominican Republic had only been a few days long, Erik and I planned on our actual honeymoon a year later. After scouring destinations, I figured Peru was the perfect place for us. While I wasn't thrilled about all of the various machines that we would come in contact with—planes, boats, and trains—I figured that sipping on pisco sours and eating guinea pigs would suffice as a distraction.

I am an extremely OCD traveler. I had designed, printed out, and coil-bound a 42-page itinerary for each of us. My itineraries are legendary and I have had many people approach me over the years to create one for their travels. I include all transportation information, tickets to historical landmarks, the most scenic and affordable Airbnbs, as well as dinner reservations at the fancy restaurants and planned lunches at the hole-in-the-wall spots. I also wanted to bring a stylish travel fanny pack on the trip but Erik threatened to divorce me if I did. Seeing as it was still early on in our marriage, I decided to save the fanny pack for another time.

Erik and I ventured across Lima, Ica, Paracas, and Cusco during our stint in Peru. We feasted on alpaca stew and roasted guinea pig until we could barely button our pants. Erik has inherited insane genes and could smoke a pack of cigarettes and still be able to walk 15 miles a day at an elevated altitude. Meanwhile, I would stretch and regularly hydrate but I would still be hobbling behind him. During our hike of Humantay Lake, our tour guide had canceled. Erik, myself, and a solo traveler named Jen were the only ones scheduled for the 6:00 AM hike. As we made our way to the base, our driver, Juan, told us not to worry and that he would walk us up there. Juan was dressed in jeans and was pushing 60. I was extremely doubtful that we would make it up.

As the hike began, my altitude sickness had started to get the better of me. On our first day at Cusco, I had thrown up and started to regularly get nosebleeds. Erik had bought me coca candy to help deal with my symptoms.

"Coca? Like cocaine? You're trying to give me cocaine candy?!"

Erik wearily rubbed his face and tried to explain the difference to me. I am infatuated with the idea of cocaine but am completely terrified of it. Given my history of love for ADHD pills, I know that cocaine is one drug I will never try, simply because I would love it too much. Also, given that I have become more of a panic-prone dweeb as I've aged, all drugs give me extreme anxiety.

Erik eventually talked me into taking the candy and I realized it had one side effect I was not prepared for: horniness. The candies were especially addicting as I rarely allow myself sweets and I convinced myself that they were basically vitamins. The first night I ate so many that we didn't have dinner until close to 11:00 PM and dessert involved something that you would see at Cirque du Soleil.

As I huffed my way up the mountain, I was gasping for air. Juan pulled out the mini oxygen tank that I had purchased and helped me breathe through it.

"You two go ahead—I take care of Miss," Juan yelled in his broken English at Erik and Jen, both of whom were hundreds of feet away.

Erik gave a semi-concerned glance back at me but I waved him away. *Let him go with Jen*, I thought to myself through wheezing breaths. *She seems single and in good shape. Maybe this is their meet-cute and I'm just the tertiary character. I hope they remember me fondly when I pass.*

Juan may have been 60, but he was in far better shape than me. He told me that he made the hike up Humantay Lake at least six times a week. He was wearing jeans and a t-shirt in 40°F along with a flimsy pair of sneakers. Despite me offering water a million times, he always declined.

"I am used to hike, Miss," he told me in a matter-of-fact way.

Hunched over and wiping my bloody nose, I lifted my head. My eyes narrowed as I took in Juan's carefree posture. Both his hands were on his hips and he looked up at the approaching lake with an expression that was equal parts stoic and smug.

I eventually did make it to the top of Humantay Lake and it was worth the excruciating altitude sickness. We got to see a live avalanche take place not far from us. The glaciers surrounding the lake still make it the most Photoshopped looking place that I have ever visited. I tipped Juan a ridiculous amount for not just being our tour guide, but also for being a fucking beast at the age of 60 and putting my 27-year-old self to shame.

When our trip came to an end, Erik and I were exhausted from all of the constant walking, hiking, eating, and drinking. As we waited in line at the airport in Lima to check our bags, I saw that the lines had exponentially grown and overhead conversations about overbooked flights. I shot Erik a worried look—while we had checked in already and had seats on the departing plane, our seats were apart. Look, despite being on numerous planes alone, including the 36+ hours of flying to Thailand and back, I am an extremely nervous passenger. If I have the option of sitting next to someone I know, then I feel like I need it (even if that person is Erik and he will spout plane facts the entire time).

As we approached the front of the line, I saw a guest service agent for Latam Airlines nearby and asked for some help. The crewmember quickly told me that the flight was overbooked and that Erik and I could not get seats together. I don't appreciate people who argue with those in the hospitality industry so I quickly nodded and let him know that I understood. As we began to shuffle away, the crewmember stopped me and told me that he could do us a favor and upgrade us. I was thrilled and graciously accepted his generous offer. At this point, a female Latam crewmember came over and started yelling at this guy in Spanish as he tried to show us to a counter for help.

I am not anywhere close to fluent in Spanish. However, I have a rare skill set where I can pick up a good amount of any foreign language when I am visiting another country. This, combined with the fact that I am from Florida and have my own Latin music playlist on Spotify, meant that I had enough knowledge to know when someone is talking about me in Spanish.

"*Es mi comisión*!" the guy barked at her.

"*No, es mio. Las americanas son mías*!" she said, wildly gesturing at us.

I was somewhat appalled that they had decided to argue about commission while assuming I wasn't Spanish and wouldn't understand them. I had been mistaken for Peruvian multiple times during our trip and spoke passable Spanish. The guy shoved her aside and ushered us to a counter. He told us that a nice lady would help us out with our upgrade and not to worry. At the Latam counter, a different crewmember went ahead and upgraded us. Just as I was feeling okay with the fact that the two previous people had been arguing over "the Americans," we were asked for a credit card. I was about to inquire why one was needed when I remembered the fight. Clearly, we had been conned into thinking this was a free upgrade. I wanted to go back and argue but Erik forked over his credit card and told me to calm down. Erik is not one to ever make a scene, even when he is wronged. I, on the other hand, was fully prepared to go tell them, in perfect Spanish, to go fuck their moms in the ass.

When we finished boarding the plane, I noticed that the plane was not even half full. I pointed out to Erik that the Latam crewmembers at the counter had clearly been telling all the passengers this in order to get commissions from upgrades that were clearly not complimentary. My blood was beginning to boil and I needed some ice cold liquor to calm me down.

The passenger in front of us, who looked like a Brazilian Barbie that had been microwaved, was yelling at the flight attendant before takeoff. She was upset that her "child" was not next to her. I looked around, expecting to see a toddler roaming the rows. Instead, I saw an extremely uncomfortable 19-year-old holding her toddler-sized luggage. Barbie insisted, loudly, that they get seats together, up front. The flight attendant explained to her that all the seats in the front of the plane were already taken and only the backseats were available (this much was true). Barbie then demanded that she get our seats since we were in the exit row and were technically closer to her daughter (whose seat was only five rows back). My face the entire time looked like I had just drank rotten milk—was this lady really demanding she be given our seats that we paid for just so she could be one row closer to her fully grown teenager?

The flight home included a brief layover in Miami. During the bumpy flight, I tried to hydrate and proceeded to chug vodka tonics. I watched Barbie chug glass of wine after glass of wine, getting more drunk and loud. Since turning 21, I have always been drunk on planes but I have never caused a scene. Barbie continuously talked about how bad the service was from the flight attendants and how horrible the wine tasted. When we hit turbulence, I got the pleasure of watching her entire glass of red wine spill on her Old Navy cardigan. I laughed out loud with glee and I am glad she turned around to see me giggling away.

By the time we landed in Miami, my bladder was bursting. The pilot announced that due to lightning, there had been delays and passengers would need to stay on the plane, taxiing, until they were given the okay to pull up to the gate. The pilot reminded us that we needed to all remain in our seats as we would not be allowed to pull up to the gate when called if passengers were walking around.

Erik and I settled in and opened up our books. I crossed my legs tightly to prevent any leakage from my urethra. We ended up taxiing for approximately 1½ hours. I can only describe what happened as ugly—*very* ugly. Passengers were all making a beeline for the bathroom. Others were asking that they be given free food and drinks to be compensated for their time. And nearly all of the passengers were constantly getting up and yelling at the flight attendants.

As I have said before, I have very little patience for people who are rude to those in the hospitality industry. I may have snapped just a little when I decided to loudly yell, "Jesus fuck. Has nobody been on a plane before? You do realize that a flight attendant has no control over this, right? What, do you think she is in charge of the FAA and is calling the shots? Newsflash: she doesn't want to be stuck in this tin can of recycled farts anymore than any of you!"

I'm not sure who heard me seeing as everyone was yelling at this point. The flight attendant, however, made eye contact and managed a weak smile. I gave her a small, dignified nod. Erik had completely ignored my outburst and was too preoccupied with guessing the queue order for the planes to approach the gates. He had been doing this for the last 45 minutes and was completely captivated. I will say, he guessed the queue orders surprisingly accurately considering there was no line and all of the planes were in a clusterfuck on the tarmac.

We eventually made it home from our journey. Latam Airlines had lost our luggage and despite numerous calls, they continued to tell me that the luggage was in Miami and that our connecting flight with American Airlines must have lost it. When I provided the tracking number to American Airlines, they showed me that the luggage had never left Lima.

I spent hours and days on the phone with Latam Airlines and was never given an apology for the lost luggage, the false complimentary upgrade, and the blatant lying from the crewmembers at the Latam counter. I sent emails and alerted their social media, but I was continuously given no help. Erik and I chose Latam as it is one of the few airlines from Orlando that goes directly to South America. Since this incident, every time we plan a vacation, I steer clear of South America. That being said, I do miss the pisco sours and I still crave roasted guinea pig. I tried to see if I could purchase the delicacy in Florida, but the employees at PetSmart were not willing to play ball.

....

In June 2018, Dadaji's health took a turn for the worse. He was in India and it was looking like he was at death's door. My parents had already been in India for several weeks when the phone call came that Dadaji's health was rapidly declining. Whenever I have known someone is dying, I have steered clear of them. Even with Mumma, the love of my life, I made every excuse possible to make visits as infrequent as possible. I had had countless family members pass away and I wasn't there when it counted—when they were scared, lonely, and their days were numbered. However, when this call came through, I immediately called Erik, told him to take a week off, and booked our tickets to India. I was going to be there when it counted.

As we boarded the Air Emirates flight, my head was pounding. While I do not feel regular empathy, I get explosive headaches when it comes to grief. The kind of headaches that render you unable to move and barely talk. When Mumma died, I am fairly sure I suffered liver damage from the amount of Tylenol I took daily. I knew that Dadaji was going to die and I had not mentally prepared for my last living link to Mumma to be gone.

As I sat down in my seat and looked for my sleep mask, I shot a look of irritation at Erik. Erik was giddy —he was on the biggest plane he had ever been on in his life and was not prepared for the Air Emirates experience. Despite that we were in coach, Erik was acting as if we each had a mini suite to ourselves. I realize I have had a very privileged life and that is why I am immune to the charms that Air Emirates economy holds (I will admit, their coach class is 1000 times better than what any other airline has to offer).

"This is a Boeing 777, Sejal!" Erik exclaimed. "Did you know it's the world's largest twin-jet plane?! And look at that wingspan!"

I tried to ignore Erik as he prattled on more facts. I put a sticker on my seat that stated not to disturb me unless it was for food. I saw out of the corner of my eye that Erik was on Facebook.

"What are you doing?" I asked.

"Well...I was going to check-in on Facebook...but then I thought it could be inappropriate..." Erik trailed off, looking sheepishly at me, the check-in status still open on his phone.

"Yeah, it would be!" I snapped, snatching his phone and exiting out of Facebook. I shoved the phone back at him and glared.

"Jeez...okay."

I couldn't believe that Erik was coming to India, of all places, with me. He had no idea what he was in for. The noise, the pollution, the staring—he was so out of his league that he was playing a completely different sport. I make it a rule to go to India only once every three to five years. Seeing as I had just been there in 2016 for wedding shopping, this was entirely too soon. As the plane took off, I took several deep breaths and reminded myself that I was being a dependable adult for once in my life.

I have no idea why I felt the need to prove that I was dependable to anyone, but this feeling was a huge driving force for me. While I always had the perfect grades and was timely to every family function, my brother was still somehow the one that the family relied on. I would like to blame this on the patriarchy and pull some feminist bullshit, but, the truth is, I was a nightmare of a child. I was the one who had bipolar disorder and that they all felt they needed to tiptoe on eggshells around. In their eyes, Marco was anchored, calm, and reliable.

Erik and I arrived in Ahmedabad at 3:00 AM. Melvin picked us up at the airport and took us to the house.

Despite sleeping during the entirety of the two flights over, plus the 12 hour layover in Dubai, I was exhausted. Since it was Erik's first time at our family home, we got the master bedroom upstairs. I went to go plug in my phone and immediately my hand got stuck to the plug, vibrating like crazy, until I was able to pull myself off. I had just been electrocuted by the outlet all because I forgot that I had to turn off the outlet's power switch before plugging anything in. I screamed very loudly and made a huge scene. Melvin decided that I did not have to go to the hospital. I glared at him as he chuckled and headed back to bed.

"Oooooh, Sejal," Erik said, opening up the weather app on his phone.

"What?" I snapped, fluffing my one inch thick pillow.

"The weather forecast tomorrow says smokey."

"Yeah. Welcome to India. That's literally the weather report for every day. Get used to it."

"Why are you in such a bad mood?"

"Gee, I don't know. Could be because Dadaji is dying. Or that I was just electrocuted. Or maybe it's the fact that I just used my parents' bathroom to brush my teeth and had flashbacks to the time I accidentally used my mom's vaginal paste as toothpaste!"

"WHAT?!"

In 2009, on a previous trip to India, I had went to parents' bathroom to brush my teeth before an early morning flight. I despise sharing toiletries but I had already packed up my belongings and did not want to look for toothpaste. I found a tube on the bathroom counter by the toothbrush holder. The tube had Hindi writing on it that I couldn't read so I proceeded to brush my teeth.

After a few seconds, I noticed that the toothpaste had a distinctly bitter, medicinal taste to it. I spit out the contents and started to gag. I grabbed my phone and used Google Translate. It turns out I mistook cream for a vaginal infection as toothpaste. To this day, the hardest part of my day is brushing my teeth and looking at myself in the mirror with an ounce of dignity.

We headed to see Dadaji at the hospital the next day. When we got to the correct hospital wing, I noticed my aunts all taking off their shoes and leaving them in a pile out front. I know this was to prevent tracking in any bacteria from the outdoors into the hospital ward, but I couldn't bring myself to walk barefoot where so many other people had. A lot of Indian shops also require you to take your shoes off outside and it is a custom that has always irked me.

Dadaji immediately had the happiest smile on his face when he saw Erik. While I am his precious princess, Dadaji was thrilled that Erik had come to India. All of my grandparents were obsessed with Erik coming to India and, despite the circumstances, it had finally happened. I got a short greeting in comparison to Erik, but I let it slide because Dadaji was glowing with excitement. The nurses came in shortly after to check on Dadaji's vitals and they reported that he seemed to be improving. Dadaji was grinning ear-to-ear. He loved nurses and anytime he had ever been to the hospital, his favorite pastime was to flirt with them. Dadaji would bat his nonexistent eyelashes and tell them that he wasn't comfortable in his bed. The nurses would fawn all over him and fuss, plumping his pillows until he was comfortable. I know it's part of a nurse's job to be polite and make patients comfortable but I have never, to this day, seen nurses dote on anyone as much as they did with Dadaji.

We visited Dadaji at the hospital every day in shifts. When it wasn't our shift, we would spend the days doing various tasks that Melvin asked of us. One of these tasks involved my brother and I opening a bank account at the local bank and getting passport photos taken. Erik was forced to also get passport photos taken.

"Why are we doing this?" Erik had asked.

"No clue," Marco responded. "Every time we come to India we always have to do some sort of errand along these lines."

The stares from the locals at Erik and I walking around together, combined with the 117°F weather, were really testing me. Ahmedabad is not a popular tourist location and therefore it's fairly uncommon to see white people there. It is even more uncommon to see a single white person walking with Indian people. This may have been the reason that Erik had become a celebrity when he went into town to get fitted for some shirts with Marco. Erik returned and told me that several little boys had asked to take pictures of him eating *paan*, a popular Indian street food. Erik then proceeded to tell me that he let them take pictures of him.

Dadaji's health began to improve and he even had a popular priest from a temple come to bless him at his bedside. Dadaji was released to go back home on his birthday. We celebrated with cake, butter chicken, and sizzlers at the house. Erik and I were leaving the next morning and I gave Dadaji the biggest hug and kiss imaginable.

....

All of his life, Dadaji just wanted people to make a fuss over him. Dadaji had lived a long life that involved tirelessly working and he was ready to sit back and be worshipped—it's one of the reasons he basked in the nurses' adoration of him. As he grew older, Dadaji wanted more attention and kisses. He wanted more Fish Filet Sandwiches and Snickers bars. He wanted the love that he always had from his friends and family to be loudly displayed.

Dadaji's condition worsened three months after our trip to India. My parents had left one September morning to go to India as Dadaji was on a ventilator. Around 10:30 AM, Pri called me.

"Hey," she said in her soft, comforting voice. "I just heard. I'm so sorry."

"Oh, about Dadaji? Yeah, he's on a ventilator. Mom and Dad just got to the airport to head there."

"Wait, what are you talking about?"

"What are you talking about?" I asked quizzically.

"Uh...that Dadaji died."

"Oh."

To all my cousins: please stop telling me you are sorry for my loss, there's a good chance I have no idea that someone has died. This was now the second time that I had been told by a cousin via phone that a grandparent passed away before I knew anything about it.

"Oh my god," Pri said regretfully. "I'm so sorry. I thought you knew."

Since I am me and I have inappropriate reactions to everything, I just broke down, laughing until tears were streaming out of my eyes.

In February, before he left for India, Dadaji kept telling us that this was the last time we would see him alive unless we came to India. Of course, we all told him to not speak like that and that we would see him in a few months. Looking back on the experience, I think two things are true: 1) Dadaji knew a lot more about his future than he let on—he was ready and happy to die and 2) He knew he wasn't dying in June and had purposely feigned illness just to get all of the family together in India, one last time. I wasn't in India for the funeral but for once I did not feel shame and regret: I knew that I had been there when it counted. I wrote the following and sent it to my aunt to be read at his funeral:

Dadaji was a businessman, a world traveler, and a beloved member of our family. In fact, we could sit here for days talking about Dadaji's many accomplishments and we would barely scratch the surface. But, what I would really like to do is talk about him as the person I remember him as. Dadaji had the best sense of humor—from the Snickers candy bars he kept in his pill dispensers to the cane he insisted "he needed," yet only used to jab us with when we were walking too slowly. One of the last conversations I had with Dadaji involved me telling him I got a new job—his immediate response was, "Really? So they interviewed you and...they liked your personality?" I kind of get the sense that he wanted to harass me just one more time.

Dadaji called all of the family's daughters and granddaughters his "princesses." He adored and doted on us endlessly (and demoted us to Princess #4 or even #9 whenever he wanted us to vie for his affection). Nobody had been more excited for me to be working towards my Doctorate in Education than Dadaji. Nearly every conversation with Dadaji that I had was about him dreaming of the moment that he would get to see his princess's name as "Dr. Madhubhai" on a diploma. You see, what Dadaji did that was really special was that he pushed his princesses—despite his years of success as a prominent businessman, Dadaji pushed his princesses to be more educated, more competitive, and more hungry for success than any other man in the room. And this in itself speaks volumes about who Dadaji was. He encouraged us to be feminine but fierce—this fire is what fuels me today.

Dadaji is the reason that our family has gotten to explore and learn from so many parts of the world. When I look back at all he has done, I can't help but think that he has lived more in one lifetime than the rest of us could possibly hope to in 100 lifetimes. I have been honored to have lived with and learned from him for the last 28 years, and I can't help but envy many of you who have had the privilege of knowing him for longer.

Losing the patriarch of your family is a profoundly existential moment. We sit here and wonder, who do we turn to now? The answer itself lies in all of us. It is now on all of us to take those many years of guidance, wisdom, and love that we have received from Dadaji and encompass that within ourselves.

10. BACK TO BROWN TOWN

In August 2018, Erik and I had been married a little over a year and had to move in with my parents. Moving in with parents when you are 27 and 33, married just a little over a year, is less than ideal. Erik had lived on his own since he was 18 and struggled to imagine living with my mom and Melvin after so many years of being independent. I had grown accustomed to having the freedom to come and go as I pleased. I knew not much would change when moving back into my parents' home and while Erik was still skeptical, he understood it was necessary.

There were many reasons for this move: my mom's struggle with alcoholism and Erik getting a promotion that would make his commute to work over one hour from where we were living were just two of the reasons. Erik and I were saving towards a house and did not want to move to the other side of town just to have to move again within a year when we purchased our home. As I was still in school and working part time, we wanted to wait until the following year to buy our home and the rent prices on the side of town by Erik's new job location were astronomical.

The other reason for the move had to deal with

me: in May of that year, I began to struggle with crippling anxiety. I could barely drive and would have to carpool with Erik to work. I started to experience blurred vision, headaches, and depersonalization. If you've never had depersonalization, then I would describe it to you like this: imagine being so high on drugs that you are experiencing everything as if you were watching it from a third-person point of view. Now imagine this happening all the time, while you are completely sober, and just trying to run errands, work, and go to school—*that's* depersonalization.

As these episodes continued, Dr. K became concerned that there could be an underlying neurological issue. Suddenly, I was whisked into the world of EEGs, MRIs, and CT scans. My neurologist told me that until the issue was resolved, I was not allowed to drive. I have rarely felt bad about my mental health diagnoses—in fact, I regularly poke fun at my bipolar disorder, anxiety, and OCD. I like to talk about this openly and lightheartedly because there is such a stigma within Asian cultures when it comes to mental health. However, when words like tumor, seizures, and brain abnormality were thrown around in front of me at doctors' offices, I started to feel defeated. Unable to drive anywhere and paralyzed from mounting anxiety and guilt, I was suddenly dependent on everyone around me.

Moving in with my parents helped to alleviate the stress that I was feeling and projecting onto other people. I was able to easily find someone to carpool with to work. My mom, who doesn't drive in general, was able to take me to my doctors' appointments and Erik did not have to take time off of work anymore. My mom and I have never had a traditionally close mother-daughter relationship but I was so grateful to have her in the house, if only to have another voice there to talk me down from my panic attacks. During this time, I gave my mom the dependency from me that she so badly craved, a dependency that she had not received from me since I was a 12.

The results of my scans revealed that I had a growth in my sinus cavity, resulting in the pressure I had been feeling in my face and my blurred vision. After being referred to an ENT, I was told that I had fluid build-up resulting from a polyp and a large cyst in my nasal sinus cavity. My initial reaction was that I had just spent months of worrying that I was dying and thousands of dollars in tests to be told that I was congested. However, once my ENT explained that I was at risk for a rupture that could potentially be life-threatening, I proceeded to schedule my surgery.

My only previous experience with anesthesia involved a colonoscopy when I was 19. As I am a self-proclaimed hypochondriac, I convinced myself that I was allergic to general anesthesia and would not wake up from the surgery. Despite that I was nearly 30, my ENT had scheduled my surgery to take place at a children's surgery center. Melvin and my mom accompanied me as I had insisted Erik not take the day off of work. I put on my brave face that morning and told Erik that I was a fighter and to remember that, if I died, I would come back as the most annoying ghost.

"Just text me when you're done," Erik sighed, shaking his head.

I was wheeled into the pre-op area where I changed into an ass-less gown and sat in a hospital bed. The first nurse came in to make sure I was comfortable before bringing my parents into the room.

"Why are they coming back here?!" I demanded, putting my hands over my starkly erect nipples that were not covered by my sheer gown.

"It's protocol," the nurse told me. "I can't take your personal items to them. They need to collect them."

My parents came barging in through the curtain and I got a view of all the toddlers I was surrounded by. *Why did they put me in a children's surgery center?!*

My mom wanted to stay with me until they wheeled me away to the operating room. I insisted that they take my clothes and my phone and go back to the waiting room. Melvin and her reluctantly agreed.

A nurse came in to start an IV on me. My entire life, I have been told that I have thin veins. I cannot count the amount of times that I have had collapsed veins due to nurses not being able to stick me. It took three nurses to find a viable vein. The third nurse did a double tourniquet and finally found one, 45 minutes after the first nurse had tried. She stuck me and all of a sudden a spray of blood squirted all over the floor, my gurney, and the nurse. I was horrified that I had just covered this woman in my bodily fluids. The nurse was a champ about it and finally got the bleeding to stop, explaining that it was just the pressure of the double tourniquet that was causing the blood to come out exploding.

For some reason I felt the need to apologize.

"I'm sorry!" I blurted out. "I know what it's like to be surprised by a gob of something that big and now that I'm on the sending end of it....I have to say, some men are really inconsiderate. On behalf of all of them, I apologize."

The nurse did not even smirk before departing the

room, carrying several blood-drenched towels with her.

Over the next 30 minutes, nurses rotated in and out of my room, pumping medicine into my IV and making me swallow pills. Anytime I asked what the medication was for, the nurse at the time would just smile and say, "Oh, just a little something to relax you, sugar!" As I was about to be wheeled off, a gorgeous African-American nurse came in. He smiled at me and offered me another round of medicine.

"Oh...the other nurse just gave me some of those I think."

He quickly glanced at my chart and then shook his head. "Nah, those are some house drugs. That's well—Imma give you top shelf."

I immediately knew that I loved this man. I quickly agreed and he injected my IV with some happy syrup as I drifted off. I was on cloud nine—I was Cookie Lyon making her triumphant return to *Empire* happy. I didn't even panic as a team of nurses rolled me towards the surgical room.

"Yo, this looks industrial as fuck," I said, still channeling my inner Cookie, as I took in the fluorescent lighting and the sterile corridors. "It looks like you're going to harvest organs here and sell them on the black market."

The nurses barely even chuckled, but I proceeded to prattle on.

"Let's talk soft lighting, are you with me?! And how about some Enya playing quietly in the background. You know, one or two small bonsai plants wouldn't kill you."

I went on to give a few other suggestions before we were in the operating room. The surgeon looked nothing like my ENT. I decided it didn't matter—I was high and happy.

"Okay," the anesthesiologist said. "Now, I want you to count backwards from 10."

Instead of listening to the anesthesiologist, I proceeded to recite Rafiki's lines from *The Lion King*, loudly singing, "*Asante sana squash banana, wewe..*"

....

Moving in with my mom and Melvin was a blessing for the most part. However, there was a learning curve that none of us were prepared for. Nobody was more excited for us to move home than my mom—she had been waiting since her children's births for one of them to come crawling back to her and this was her chance! My surgery was a success but full recovery took nearly six weeks for me as I refused to take my pain pills. I was in constant pain and my mom was fully enjoying my slow recovery.

My mom loves her children more than anything. While she might love Marco a bit more, she is deeply obsessed with us and loves to feel needed. My mom's greatest calling in life was to be a homemaker. Marco rarely visits home and when he does, he uses my mom to fetch him chai and deliver it to his bed. I rarely ask my mom for help with anything and she was delighted that I was too weak to do anything the first few days after my surgery.

When we first got home and I stumbled my way to the bathroom, my mom quickly followed me. There was a look of pure glee as she pulled down my pants and sat me on the toilet. I'm happy to report that I was able to wipe by myself, but that's not to say that my mom didn't unspool the toilet paper as she manically looked on, waiting to be called for more assistance. I am fairly certain that part of the reason for my long recovery time was that my mom was *Misery*-ing me—I was James Caan and she was my brown Kathy Bates.

My mom is not smart in the traditional way but she has many skills that I will never acquire. For one, she is a couponing savant. My mom knows the exact price of a gallon of milk at Walmart versus Publix versus CVS Pharmacy. She can do math *Good Will Hunting* fast when it comes to calculating if it is cheaper to buy the squash you pick out by hand or the prepackaged squash. My mom also cooks every type of cuisine and always nails it—Indian, Chinese, Mexican, Italian, she can cook it all.

However, since my mom did not grow up in America, she lived a fairly sheltered life after marriage. That is until my brother and I grew older and started to teach her various phrases. I once mentioned that I wanted to have a threesome with two characters in a Bollywood movie. My mom had absolutely no idea what this meant, so she proceeded to laugh.

"Do you know what a threesome is?" I asked, already knowing the answer.

"No...what is threesome?"

I never told her and it drove her absolutely mad. These are the kinds of things I thoroughly enjoy taunting my mom with. A few years later, my mom came home from her job at Macy's. Marco and I were on the patio and she quickly joined us with a sheepish expression.

"We were talking about lesbians at work," she told my brother. "Do you know what is ding dong?"

There was a brief moment of silence before my brother and I began to howl like banshees. Marco and I are like two jackals when we laugh. We both have a high pitch cackle and they sync up together. Both of us usually fall on the floor, clutching our stomachs, half crying and half laughing, as drool steadily streams from our mouths.

"Do you mean dildo?" Marco finally managed to ask, trying to catch his breath.

"*What?*" Melvin said, overhearing this as he came outside to see what all the fuss was about. "What's going on out here?!"

"Yeah! Dildo!" my mom exclaimed, her eyes lighting up at the thought that she was about to expand her English vocabulary.

"Ask Dad!" Marco said.

My mom looked pleadingly at me and I shook my head. "I'm staying far out of this. Melvin, would you care to take this one?"

"Guys, that's enough," Melvin said, trying to hide a smirk as he attempted to be serious. He then shot my mom a furtive look and quietly added, "I'll tell you later."

This truly embodies who my mom is: she is always a good sport when we laugh at her expense but she is surprisingly open-minded and always wants to be in on the joke. My mom has had her shortcomings but she makes up for it with love and a lot cursing in English with a heavy Indian accent—*nothing* makes me smile quite like when my mom curses.

Erik had always been used to my mom being a sweet homemaker and hearing her curse has given him pure joy since we moved in. Erik loves my mom more than I do, which is fine since my mom loves Erik more than anyone else, living or dead. Since moving in, my mom will deliver Erik's food to our room, on a table, and place it next to him while he plays Xbox. She even has a platter plate designated just for him. I think the whole arrangement is ridiculous but then again, my mom will always do whatever she wants.

One such example is when Erik bought a new car. My mom wanted to do a traditional blessing with the car, which involves a coconut and drawing red swastikas. I pointed out that Erik was going to have to leave his car unattended at work in a predominantly multi-ethnic neighborhood and maybe the coconut and swastikas weren't a great idea.

"Hmm. Right," my mom responded. "Okay, no coconut. Just swastikas."

Before we could stop her, my mom painted two bright red swastikas on Erik's dark green car. Erik was a good sport about it up until a few weeks later when we were driving through a Hispanic neighborhood. Our German Shepherd started to ferociously bark at two men walking by the car as we were at a stoplight.

"*Nein*! *Ruhig*!" we both shouted.

It was at this moment, as we were both shouting German commands to our dog, with Erik looking like the master of the Aryan race with his blonde hair and blue eyes, that we decided it was time to wash away the swastikas before his car got bashed.

My mom was okay with us washing away the swastikas but that has never stopped her from drawing swastikas on our doorstep during the month leading up to Diwali. This is coincidentally also right around the time that Halloween happens. I never question why we get so few trick-or-treaters. At first, it was the swastikas alone—now, it's the swastikas combined with our terrifyingly loud dog that we scream at in German commands.

The one thing that my mom hasn't gotten her way

with is forcing me to wear a bra. Since moving back home, my mom had noticed—but stayed quiet about—me frequently not wearing a bra. One day, I came home wearing a modest pink dress but my nipples were fully visible through the sheer fabric.

"Why don't you wear bra?" she demanded.

"Why? Does that make you...uncomfortable?" I asked, a smile slowly spreading across my face. I started to slowly shimmy, working my shoulders so that my asymmetrical c-cups were jiggling.

"Sejal...stop it."

My mom started to run away from me and I decided to start taunting her by using my teamster voice voice and saying, "Hey, BB. Look at my thangs jiggle."

I eventually proceeded to leave my mom alone and retreated to my room, wanting her to feel safe. When I heard her go down the hallway, I immediately went into the kitchen and took my left boob out. My mom came towards the kitchen and asked me why I was giggling.

"Oh...because...the burritos!" I panicked and named the first food item I saw next to me, which just happened to be my signature two burritos from Chipotle.

As my mom rounded the corner, I popped out from the open refrigerator door and yelled, "HEY BB!"

My mom immediately screamed and then yelled, "Gross!"

"Well, that was rather rude," I said, tucking my left boob back into my tank top.

"How would you feel if I do that to you?" she snapped.

"Well, your boobs are obviously gross. You're almost 60 and they're already deflated from having two babies gnaw on them 30 years ago!"

My mom and I have a confusing relationship to say the least. The only hobby, if you can even call it that, we have in common is that we love to feed other people. We have very little in common outside of food. However, when we are not driving each other insane with our screaming and she is not succumbing to her alcoholism, we get along surprisingly well. I enjoy the fact that my mom is a mix of traditional with a splash of the unexpected. My mom is difficult to accept but easy to love. I think this rings true for most children of addicts—we love them unconditionally but often neglect this fact because we find it arduous to accept them for all of their shortcomings.

While my mom was the first to be against my relationship with Erik, she has since grown to revere him like some sort of God—Erik eats spicier food than anyone in the family and he eats more Indian food than I do, easily making him her favorite family member. After nearly 50 years on Earth, my mom finally learned that skin color is the least important thing when it comes to choosing a spouse. She has accepted that her daughter is very different than what she had dreamed for, yet loves me anyways. My mom has learned that she is deeply flawed and sometimes fails to acknowledge that, in spite of this, she is still profoundly loved. Most importantly, though, my mom has learned that steaks are delicious and that smoking weed is fun.

....

Melvin is a saint. I would never say this to his face for fear of him lording it over me for the rest of my life, but the man is heaven sent. Melvin cleared out the entire master bedroom for us to move into. He went car shopping with Erik and I to make sure that the salesman at the dealership understood they were dealing with a grumpy, miserly Indian man who wanted every discount possible. Melvin even let me get a dog, despite that he had been opposed to it for years. Every single friend who has met Melvin has told me that they wish he was their dad.

Don't be misled by the above doting—Melvin is seriously flawed and I let him know it. We are very similar in that we both love reading, adventures, trying new food, and binging British crime serials. However, my dad is insanely positive and I am the complete opposite. Melvin is the kind of guy who wakes up at 5:00 AM on a Saturday just to smell wet grass and listen to the morning birds while he drinks his coffee.

"Isn't this wonderful?" Melvin sang, his normally beady eyes all wide and happy.

"No," I said flatly. I had woken up early for a doctor's appointment and I hated every part of it. "The nauseating stench of the lawn is burning my nose and why won't those birds shut up?"

"Aw, Sejal, this is what it's all about! Breathe in that morning air and listen to the birds chirping." Melvin, feeling as if I needed a demonstration on how to breathe and not turn off my ears, closed his eyes and took in a loud, deep breath, perking his head slightly up.

"I'm going inside. This is gross."

Melvin's incessant glass-half-full personality has always irritated me and I constantly look for ways to make his life a little darker.

Two weeks before Mumma died, we were headed home from visiting her at the hospital. My dad, listening to a football game, had the radio on full blast and was driving at least 20 over the speed limit. As we approached an intersection, Melvin slammed on the breaks.

"Dammit! I'm going to miss the end of this game. Look at all these cars!"

"Uh...that's a funeral procession," I pointed out.

"Oooooh, good idea, Sej!" Melvin said in a scheming sort of voice. He gunned it and joined in at the middle of the procession, turning on his hazard lights.

"That wasn't a suggestion!" I shouted. "Are we seriously tailgating a funeral procession right now?"

Look, I don't believe in karma. I'm not saying that Melvin killed my grandmother. I'm just saying that he chose to pretend to be a part of a funeral procession in order to make it home to watch the Miami Dolphins lose, like always...and then, two weeks later, on the dot, my grandmother died.

When Mumma passed away, I became very fond of her bonsai trees. I hate flowers but something about these trees in miniature has always been therapeutic for me. I would help Mumma to water the plants every day. After she passed away, I kept up with this tradition of watering and pruning the plants. When I moved out, I instructed Melvin that he needed to ensure that the plants were kept in prime condition.

A few months after moving out, I came home one day to notice the bonsai trees weren't at their usual spot by the windowsill.

"What happened to the bonsais?" I asked.

Melvin gave me a sheepish expression. "Oh... well...they weren't really surviving."

"What do you mean?"

"I wasn't watering them and they died!"

"Did you throw them away?"

"No..."

"Where are they?" I demanded. I was not in the mood for Melvin's riddles.

Melvin walked out to the back patio and I followed. He opened a steel cabinet next to his barbecue grill and then pulled out two brown plants.

"What?! You shoved them in there?"

"Well, I didn't want to throw them away so... yeah."

I looked at the brittle branches and the sand that resembled sawdust. If he had told me sooner, I could have repotted them and saved them! I shoved the disheveled plants back into the steel cabinet and proceeded to march out of the house.

I waited a few days until my mom was out of town to exact my revenge. I rarely will blatantly do something retaliatory—I am more partial to mind games. I went to my parents' house while Melvin was at work. It was pouring outside and I was quick to take my shoes off on the front porch and pull a towel out of my bag. I had come prepared. I toweled off and stealthily entered the house. First, I decided to bring the garbage bins in from outside. I opened the garage and dragged them in, perfectly aligning them in an orderly fashion.

I then dried myself off with a second towel I brought and went to the back porch. I retrieved the dead bonsai trees and brought them inside, ostentatiously placing them on the dining room table. I wiped any wet footprints with a third towel, dragging it behind me as I made my exit.

Later that evening, Melvin texted me. I had been preparing for this moment.

Melvin: Hey, did you come to the house today?
Me: No. I went to work and just got home.
Melvin: Weird. Are you sure? Someone brought the trash bins inside the garage.
Me: Bringing in trash bins? Does that even remotely sound like something that I would do?
Melvin: Let me check with Missy.

Melvin disappeared from the text for a solid 10 minutes, presumably to talk to our neighbor, Missy. I silently prayed that Missy had not seen me

Melvin: Okay, this is really strange. Missy said she didn't do it.
Me: I don't know.
Melvin: Now I am freaking out. The bonsai plants are on the dining room table!
Me: Weird. Maybe Mumma's ghost is finally haunting you for killing her bonsai trees.
Melvin: Haha. Very funny.
Me: I'm serious. It's bad enough you killed her by pretending to be part of a funeral procession just to make it home for a game. Now you've killed her plants.

I let Melvin believe he was being haunted by Mumma's ghost for several weeks before coming clean. The mystery drove him mad and was the only subject that he discussed until I confessed to being the garbage bin/bonsai bandit. Nothing in this world gives me the same joy as reveling in Melvin's misery. That's not to say he doesn't deserve it. Besides being ridiculously chipper all the time, Melvin is also insanely oblivious.

A few months after moving back home, Melvin and I were on our own for dinner. My mom had gone down south to visit Marco and Erik was working. Melvin was still on a phone call with his boarding school buddy so I sat down at the dining table to eat alone. I had cooked up a juicy New York strip and I was ready to reap the rewards of my hard labor.

I took a few bites and I was in heaven—the steak was simply succulent and paired well with my $2.99 Trader Joe's Cabernet Sauvignon. As I went in for a fourth bite, I suddenly froze. The steak had become lodged in my throat and I was choking. I tried to suck in air and couldn't breathe. I patted myself on the back in a vain attempt to dislodge the meaty morsel. I stood up and frantically started waving my arms around. Melvin briefly made eye contact with me before chuckling at something his friend had said and continuing his call.

At this point, it had been approximately 30 seconds since I had taken my last breath of air and I started to panic. I made the international choking sign and Melvin still only looked vaguely interested. I finally hurled myself against the edge of the couch, which slid several feet away on the wooden floor. The momentum of this knocked me to my knees and I immediately threw up the full piece of steak that I had been choking on, as well as the rest of the dinner I had consumed prior to that. I gasped for air and my arms were shaking. Drool and vomit dripped down from my bottom lip, pooling on the floor.

"Uh, hang on one sec," Melvin said into the phone before covering the receiver and looking at me. "Sej, you okay?"

"I WAS CHOKING, YOU BASTARD!"

"Well, how would I know that?" Melvin earnestly said before returning to his call.

Stubborn as always, Melvin refused to admit any wrongdoing for several days. When my mom came home, I was quick to regale her with the episode. My mom spent the next 24 hours shooting Melvin the same death stare that I had been giving him. Melvin finally apologized for his lack of good timing and intervention.

Unfortunately for Melvin (and myself), this would not be the last time that year that he had poor timing. A month later, I had decided to surprise Erik with some new lingerie. As Erik and I were headed to the bed, we could hear our dog starting to cry from her crate.

"Did you cover the crate up?" I asked, pulling down Erik's pants.

Erik gave me an uncertain look.

"Wait right here," I instructed his penis.

Since it was nearly 2:00 AM, I decided it was safe to venture out 15 feet from our room to check on the dog's crate. I went behind the crate and pulled the sheet down, quietly shushing the puppy in a soothing tone. All of a sudden, a blinding white light came into my face.

"What the..."

"AHHHHHHHH!" I screamed.

Melvin was roaming the pitch black halls and had shined his flashlight directly on me. Now, listen, I'm sure you are thinking that this can't possibly be *that* bad—trust me, it was. I was in fishnet stockings and whore-level bedazzled stilettos. I had on a see-through bustier that snapped open at the crotch. This was worse than if I had been caught naked—in fact, I would have preferred to have been caught naked.

"I didn't see anything!" Melvin immediately shouted, backing away and fumbling with his phone as he hit a nearby wall in his attempt to flee. "I didn't see anything!!!"

I returned to the room and Erik took in my frazzled demeanor and slatternly state. Erik is almost completely deaf in one ear. If a murderer was hacking me to pieces while we were sleeping, I would be surprised if my screams would even make Erik slightly twitch. When I told him what had happened, Erik looked completely mortified.

"I've never said this before in my life, but...Erik, I'm not in the mood."

"Me either."

I normally sleep in the nude but after this incident, we both put on sweats and laid in bed, keeping at least two feet of distance between us at all times. The next day, I actively avoided any contact with my parents. My mom tried to bring up the incident and I quickly shut it down. I was determined to act like nothing had happened. Melvin had a different plan.

"Hey, Sej!" he quickly stopped me as I tried to make a beeline from the kitchen to my room.

"Yeah?" I said, trying to sound as casual as possible.

"So, uh, you know," he started, already looking flustered and trying to stifle a laugh. "Last night...I, uh, I didn't see anything."

"Oh my god."

I went to my room and hid under the covers in shame. Whenever someone has to repeatedly tell you that they didn't see anything, that is a clear sign that they saw *everything*. I remained celibate for nearly a week after this incident. Somehow, Melvin was less traumatized than me. A few days later, him and my mom were going on a trip to visit Marco. Before leaving, Melvin gave a smile and slyly said, "Enjoy. You guys will have the house to yourselves."

I think part of the reason that Melvin was less disturbed by the late-night lingerie sighting is because he has been praying for grandchildren from day one. While my mom desperately wants grandchildren, she has never actively pushed me towards it. Melvin, on the other hand, tried everything to get Erik and I to give him those blue-eyed, Wheat Thin colored grandchildren that he wanted so badly. When it's tax season, Melvin would calculate how much money we would get back instead of owing if we had a child. When I mention how much I want to travel, Melvin immediately offers up free babysitting while Erik and I travel the world. And, my favorite, when I comment on how cute my cousin Anisha's baby is, Melvin is the first to jump in and tell me that I could also have a really cute baby.

"Imagine, Sej! Your dark hair with Erik's light blue eyes. And, you know, the baby would probably have a very nice complexion."

"Okay, plot twist: the baby is born very pale but with all of my dark facial and body hair. Oh, and the baby has my tar-colored eyes."

"Hmm," Melvin said, letting me know that he was disgruntled.

Erik and I are constantly asked about when we are having kids. Listen to me and listen good: we do not want any kids. Every time we say that, people say that we will change our minds. No, we won't, because we are adults, we know ourselves and what we want, and kids are just not a part of that. I find children to be incredibly annoying from the ages of three to 23. They are horrible conversationalists and they don't understand that I want to drink my martini alone in peace. Erik and I are not rich by any stretch of the imagination, but whatever money we have to spend, we like to spend on dinner with our couples friends, booking exotic vacations, and expanding our wine collection. Kids do not fit into our budget.

Erik and I have been together for seven years and we have thoroughly discussed the topic of children. There are three scenarios under which we have agreed that we will have a child:

1. If I am dying, I will make sure to have a surrogate carry our child. The primary reason for this is because Erik cannot take care of himself —he gets so wrapped up in work that he completely falls apart alone. He needs a woman and Erik, by himself, is not marketable. Erik as a single, young widow with an attractive mixed-race baby? Now, *that* is marketable.
2. If Erik is dying, I will be the first to inseminate myself. I really don't like dating and have no reason to get married or even pursue a relationship if Erik is dead. A baby would give my empty life meaning. Moreover, I would just love all of the sympathy that I would get from people for being a young widow who is also a single mother. That sympathy would afford me to take all the exotic vacations I desired while dumping the baby at my parents' house until it was old enough to have a cocktail.
3. If Erik and I become filthy rich, I will have a baby. Having children and looking flawless is really easy if you are rich—you can get a nanny, a dietician, and a personal trainer. I would prefer a sur-

rogate because I cannot imagine going 40 weeks without oysters, sushi, and wine. However, I am open to the sacrifice as long as Erik is willing to pay for my vaginal rejuvenation following the birth. Pregnant women can still take Xanax, right?

EPILOGUE: REASONS WHY ERIK WANTS TO DIVORCE ME

I am not easy to be married to. I will clean, cook, run errands, and organize everything in the house. I will pay bills and manage the budget. I will keep stock of all of your toiletries so you never run low on deodorant and body wash. I will never make boring dinner plans and I will regularly blow you.

With all that said, I have a wildcard personality. I have the temperament of a cat—I don't like attention in general but when I want it, I will suffocate you with it. I constantly think that I am dying from some sort of illness and have frequent panic attacks that I need to be talked out of. I stick to a strict snacking and napping schedule—anytime I stray from this schedule, I become extremely fussy and I end up reverse cycling. At best, I am a hypochondriac toddler.

The title of this chapter was inspired by a hashtag I began from when we first got married. There are many reasons over the years why Erik wants to divorce me—whether it's the fact that I iron my cash (with starch) or that I steal any loose change at my parents' house even though I'm almost thirty. It could also be because I came home after my fifth laser hair removal and told Erik, "I feel so smooth, like a dolphin! Feel it!" I then proceeded to do my best dolphin impersonation, which somehow killed the mood. As you can see, there are a lot of reasons for Erik to divorce me. However, so as to not give away all of my bad habits, I've rounded up some of his top reasons below:

Gone Girl: A Love Story

Erik and I had the fun task of sorting through 150 invitations for our wedding and stuffing all of the invites with the various event cards. I decided that the perfect movie to play while preparing for our wedding was *Gone Girl.* As I hummed with a big smile on my face, Erik gave me a look of concern.

"You know, I don't feel like what Amy did was so wrong."

"You're joking, right?" Erik rubbed his eyes.

"Look, her husband was a dick. Like, Nick was cheating with Emily Ratajkowski. Granted, yes, she is insanely hot—but her character is a bimbo! Amy was *Amazing Amy*!"

"Sejal, she framed her husband for her death."

"Right...but she did it for a good reason. Let's not forget, they just showed Nick shoving her in that flashback!"

"So, in your mind, infidelity and one shove means that it's acceptable to ruin someone's life?"

"Yes," I immediately said. I continued to hum and stuff the invitations before leaning over to give Erik a kiss on the cheek. "This is my happy place."

I am not a romantic person by nature. I have spoken to my therapist multiple times about my inability to understand why what I think is romantic just isn't romantic. To me, movies like *Gone Girl* are the perfect date night movie because it's a thriller but it's also a love story. I have been assured by my therapist, as well as the general public, that *Gone Girl* is definitely not a love story. Until Gillian Flynn tells me this herself, I refuse to believe it.

On another occasion, Erik and I were sitting on the bed, just casually watching a rerun of *The Office*. Suddenly, I became overcome with affection. I turned to aggressively and forcibly kiss him.

"What was that?" Erik asked, pulling away with a disgusted look on his face.

"I was being romantic!"

"Seriously?" Erik asked, wiping his lip as he checked for signs of bleeding.

"What?!" I whined. "I saw it in that romantic comedy!"

"Which one? You don't even watch rom-coms!"

"The one with Mark Wahlberg and Reese Witherspoon! You know, where they're teenagers in love."

"Sejal…that movie is called *Fear* and it is about an abusive boyfriend."

"Well…there were good times, too! He fingered her on a rollercoaster…that's very romantic, Erik."

Erik Hid The Body

In 2013, When Erik and I first started hanging out regularly, there were maybe three other people in the world who knew about it. Since Erik was my boss at the time, we were careful to only go to Erik's apartments or to dive bars in the middle of nowhere if we wanted to go out. I would lie to my parents about my whereabouts and the only people who would occasionally know that I was meeting Erik were Lizzy and Lauren.

As I have previously pointed out, I truly spent most of my young adult life believing that the majority of men I met were serial killers. Erik and I were so secretive in the months leading up to us actually becoming "official" that it would have been impossible for anyone else to know that we were dating. After two weeks of this, it dawned on me that something could happen to me and nobody would ever know where I last was. I was on my way to meet Erik for a cocktail at his apartment and I began to panic.

Erik is charming, good looking, and ridiculously smart, I thought to myself. *But so was Ted Bundy...*

I pulled out my phone at the next traffic light and quickly opened up my notes. I proceeded to open a new note and write in, "Erik hid the body." The note had the time and date stamp on it. I quickly emailed it to myself and saved it under a folder that backed up to my laptop at home. I breathed a sigh of relief knowing that if Erik tried to off me, there would be serious repercussions.

I proceeded to do this for the first seven months of our relationship. Once we went public with our relationship and enough people knew, I deleted this note. I proudly let Erik know how I, a commitment-phobic, crime-thriller-watching woman, had made this huge step.

"You had a note in your phone that accused me of murder?" Erik asked, appalled.

"I don't know why you're surprised," I said nonchalantly. "Nobody knew we were dating and could vouch for my whereabouts when I was with you. I had to make sure that if you were planning on offing me, the police could trace it back to you."

"*Offing* you? Good grief, Sejal, this isn't *Goodfellas*. What if you had been murdered by someone else and then I got blamed for it?"

I thought about this for a second before saying, "Well, then, you would go to prison. Honestly, though, you would be fine there."

"I would be *fine* in prison?"

"You're cute and would make a wonderful boyfriend to one of the more gruff guys there. You would instantly have protection. You might have to tattoo a set of tits on your back, but, in all reality, that's not the worst thing. You would have more time to focus on your reading there!"

Erik glared daggers at me for several days. I never felt bad about my decision to do this and, in August of that year, my choice was further validated by the Goddess that is Chrissy Teigen. Chrissy tweeted that she always kept a note in her pocket that said. "John did it," in the event that she is killed. While Chrissy's motivation was purely to prevent John from remarrying, and not out of fear that he might be a serial killer, I sense that she is a kindred spirit and provided me with the validation that I didn't know I needed. Erik, on the other hand, sensed that he now hated both me and Chrissy Teigen. I made it clear to him that I would not stop worshipping my Chrissy Teigen shrine and that we needed to increase our offering to her statue to at least five additional chicken wings a day.

This Is My Mom

One evening, Erik and I were having a glass of wine with Elsie on our back patio. As the night proceeded, a glass of wine turned into three bottles of wine and the conversation had started to turn emotional and deep. I am not an emotional drunk. I enjoy alcohol for its taste and am more silly than anything. Erik and Elsie were starting to talk about their childhoods and were having a deep conversation about events that had traumatized them.

Erik started to tell a story that to this day makes me laugh harder than anything else. Erik had been in elementary school and they were holding an event in the classroom where all of the parents came in to talk about their jobs. Erik's mom was a beast and was working several jobs while going to college full-time. As such, she didn't have time to go to this event and her boyfriend at the time dropped Erik off at school.

As the students each took turns proudly introducing their parents, Erik began to get upset. He told the teacher his mom hadn't been able to come. The teacher was sweet to him and offered to go up with him so that Erik could talk to everyone about his mom's jobs. Erik, completely misunderstanding the purpose of the teacher coming up with him, went to the front of the classroom and sobbed, "I'm Erik...a-and, this is my mom!" Erik then gestured at the confused looking teacher as he continued to cry.

This story absolutely slayed me. I literally fell on the floor of the patio and was gasping for air. I clutched at my chest trying to stop myself but the laughter was uncontrollable. After several minutes of flopping around on the ground like a beached dolphin, I finally caught my breath and looked up. Elsie and Erik were looking at me with both of their jaws hanging open.

"What is wrong with you?" Elsie finally asked. "You're a monster."

In case you are wondering, I am fully aware of what a monster I am. I have already stated before that I have very inappropriate reactions to grief and just sadness in general. I don't like feeling sad so I use humor and suppression to deflect sadness. I definitely don't understand when other people look back on traumatic events and fail to see the humor in them. To this day, I frequently share this story with others to try to get them to realize why I find this story so funny. The only person who has agreed with me is Marco and that's because, as Erik puts it, he is a jackal, just like me.

Valentine's Day

Erik and I loathe Valentine's Day. Even if I hadn't always hated the holiday, something about working in the restaurant industry for so many years on end makes you extremely jaded when it comes to Hallmark holidays. Perhaps it was all of the awful proposals we had been subjected to for years. When will people learn that proposing by putting your ring inside of food is not romantic?

On one such occasion, I had a guest insist that the engagement ring be put at the bottom of a champagne flute to be delivered to the table. I pointed out that this was a choking hazard and due to liability issues, we could not do this. I also told him that his soon-to-be fiancée would not want her ring to be sticky from the alcohol and her having to spit out her new ring.

"Oh, good point," the guest said. "Okay, let's go ahead and stick the ring on the tail of the shrimp cocktail."

Sticking rings inside of cake or champagne I can almost understand. But seafood? On the tail of a shrimp? It's bad enough to be taken to a mediocre local restaurant that hasn't been renovated in 20 years on Valentine's Day. The only worse thing is being proposed to at said ancient restaurant with a ring that is essentially on the butt of a crustacean and now smells like shrimp.

When the couple arrived for the reservation that evening, the only table we had left was a two-person booth. These booths have roughly two feet of bench on each side. Since no other tables were available, they took the booth and insisted on sitting next to each other. As much as I hate restaurant proposals, I hate couples who sit on the same side of the booth even more. This man's bride-to-be was not petite, to say the least, resulting in her future fiancé sitting with ¼ of a buttcheek on the booth's bench and the rest of his body awkwardly hanging out.

When the shrimp cocktail arrived and the moment came for him to propose, he got down on one knee and told a long speech. He had tears in his eyes and finally asked her to marry him. She had the most bored expression on her face and after a solid 10 seconds, she finally jutted out her left hand, gave a curt nod as she pursed her lips and said, "Mhm." Her fiancé broke down in sobs and kissed her unenthused face, smiling brightly while she continued to frown. I still believe that he would have gotten a more enthusiastic response if he had not sat next to her, had not used a cocktail shrimp as the ring holder, and, most importantly, if he had not proposed to her on Valentine's Day.

When we were dating, Erik and I made it a point to purposely avoid seeing each other on Valentine's Day out of protest for the absurd holiday. Since we no longer worked together, this was fairly easy. However, once we were married and living together, this was no longer an option.

In 2019, I decided to throw Erik for a curveball. I told him that I had gotten him an extra special Valentine's Day. While he was at work, I set the mood by dimming the lights, playing soft music, and lighting some candles. I prepared a martini for him and wrote a meaningful card. I then wrapped his present in an attractive, Valentine's Day themed gift bag. I sat in the darkness and sipped my martini, patiently waiting for him to come home like a spider waits for a fly to come into its web.

"Come here," I called from the living room when Erik arrived at 12:30 AM. "No traps."

Erik tried to look pleased that I had done something for the special holiday, but even I could see the underlying disgust that his face was unable to hide. Erik eyed the martini suspiciously as I repeated, "No traps," and handed him his present.

When Erik opened the bag, he realized that the "present" was a laminated certificate from the Hemsley Conservation Centre. I had named a cockroach after Erik at the conservatory and there was now a plaque with his full name on it. Erik took in all of the production value that I had put into this charade—the lights, cocktails, candles, music, decorations, etc.

"Are you serious right now?" Erik asked.

"Yes!" I trilled. "Now when I'm mad at you and call you a miserable little cockroach, it will *literally* be true.

Wine Lockdown

I love wine. I am basically like a reverse Jesus—you know that trick where he turns water into wine? Well, I turn my wine into water by ensuring that it hydrates me and never betrays me for a hangover. Erik's love of wine was one of his most attractive features—his knowledge of wine greatly surpasses that of anyone I have met. While I can appreciate fine wine, I am also more than content with drinking Trader Joe's Cabernet Sauvignon. I like to think of it as balance.

One night, after a particularly egregious day at work, I put on my robe and crawled into bed.

"Erik, can you get me a glass of wine?"

"Uh, okay. I didn't buy any at the store today. Do you want me to open one from our collection?"

"No, just grab a glass! I have an emergency bottle in the nightstand!"

"...What? Where? Why?"

"ERIK. It's in *your* nightstand. And it's for EMERGENCIES."

Erik proceeded to give me a disgusted look as he retrieved a bottle of wine, whose existence he had previously been unaware of, from his nightstand. He begrudgingly poured the wine.

A few months later, I came home to a padlock on the wine cage.

"Why is all of the good wine looked up in my wine cage?" I immediately asked Erik.

"Well, first off, it's *our* wine cage—it was a wedding present, remember? Second of all, it's locked because your friends come over and I come home to multiple bottles open. You've also alluded to the fact that you want the option of drinking the good stuff without saving me any."

"Well...where's my key?"

"There's only one key and I have it on my keychain."

"B-b-but...what if there's an emergency and my nightstand wine is out of stock?!"

Erik shook his head in disgust and walked away with the wine key. I started to Google how alimony payments worked in the state of Florida and if I could get by on that. The above most likely falls under reasons that I want to divorce Erik.

....

If you've made it this far, then you are probably wondering how I am still married. Clearly, there are a lot of reasons to divorce me. I am stubborn, obnoxious, and very demanding when it comes to my wine. Everyone is constantly telling me how lucky I am to have Erik in my life and, to be honest, it pisses me off. Would it kill them, just once, to mention how lucky Erik is to have me in his life? Neel is the only person in my family who constantly reminds Erik of this fact and threatens him with violence should he ever upset me, two things that I am very grateful for.

Erik is the kind of guy who waves and claps for free stuff from a t-shirt cannon at a basketball game. Erik is also the kind of guy who loves pirate dinner adventures and wants to go to every interactive dining experience with mediocre food. Erik eats chicken wings from a box and then proceeds to leave the empty bones in with the remaining wings. All of these are reasons to deem Erik as being very suspect. However, the worst thing about Erik is that his love of nerdy things far outweighs mine, almost to an obnoxious degree.

It was 3:46 AM and Erik had been in bed watching videos about magnetars for the last 30 minutes. I was extremely annoyed and Erik kept explaining, out loud might I mention, "fun" facts to me. Did I mention that this was on my birthday?

"So. This is what you're doing tonight?" I asked flatly, gesturing to my lingerie.

"Oh my god. This is amazing, Sejal!" Erik cooed, not even throwing a glance in my direction.

I tied my hair up in a messy bun and pulled down my sleep mask after I turned on the TV to a rerun of *The Office*. I sat there and happily thought about ways that I could still frame Erik for murder.

As I made a mental note to look up life insurance policies in the morning, I turned around and gave Erik a kiss on the cheek before sweetly saying, "Goodnight."

DEDICATION

There are so many people without whom this book would not be possible. First and foremost, I would like to thank my family—I'm really sorry there isn't a redacted version of this book available. Erik, you were there for me every step of the way during the writing process and supplied me with endless wine as I typed away at all hours of the day, dressed like a homeless person.

Cory Fisher, you have always been so supportive and I could not have made it through the editing process without you. Thank you for letting me always say, "There are barely any typos in this chapter," and never telling me, "I told you so," when my wine-induced writing haze led to sentences that I couldn't even understand.

Chelsea Parrish Chana, you were an absolute gem to work with and made my vision for this cover photo come to life. From the moment I started writing, I told everyone that you were the only photographer I would work with. This book would not have been the same without your superb photography skills. Thank you for making me look like I have the requested "Gollum arms" that I kept insisting on.

Juliana Correa, who would have thought that when I met you over 15 years ago that you would one day be designing my book cover? Your patience for my requests clearly has no bounds. The minute I wrote this book,

I knew I needed your graphic designing skills on this. Thank you for being so talented.

Royce and Marie, you guys won't believe how much cum can fit on these pages! You two always made sure that I at least ate every weekend instead of just being glued to my laptop while boozing it up—for that, and the booze you supplied, I am very grateful.

Last, but certainly not least, a sincere, heartfelt thank you to Trader Joe's for making such delicious wine. Just know that your Cabernet Sauvignon fueled the majority of the writing on these pages.